■ REVOLUTION IN COUNSELING:

Implications of Behavioral Science

Edited by **John D. Krumboltz**
Stanford University

Major papers presented at the 1965
Cubberley Conference at Stanford University

HOUGHTON MIFFLIN COMPANY · BOSTON

New York · Atlanta · Geneva, ILL.
Dallas · Palo Alto

FOREWORD

Counselors are inclined to be concerned and warm-hearted about their clients, and to be dedicated to helping them. This is an essential characteristic, but it is easy for empathy to become sympathy and for counselors to work *for* the student and not with him. Their emotions may cloud their cognitive function almost to the degree that this is true for their clients. Yet it is all-important that the counselor really care for his client, and that he be able to communicate this sense of caring. Counselors are inclined also to have large goals for counseling, global rather than specific, ultimate in Byrne's sense, and unattainable directly rather than immediate and observable as behavior outcomes. Counselors worry about these matters of sympathy and idealism, yet do not know how to translate them into specific counselor behaviors and client outcomes. The authors of the first two chapters in this volume think that they can help counselors to make the translation, perhaps even to substitute specifics for generalities, by using the evidence and methods of behavioral scientists. They make their case with assurance and evidence. The next two writers are not sure that this is more than a partial answer, though they acknowledge the validity of the partial. One even thinks that the revolution of behaviorism in counseling puts the cart before the horse. We would admit, I think, that it is a better cart. The last chapter is an attempt to recapitulate the argument and to effect a degree of reconciliation. Most of all it is a plea for tolerance of new and uncomfortable ideas and for recognition of the worth of the "opposition" no matter which point of view one currently supports.

This small book represents a revolution in that it is the first major attempt to propose systematically the application of behaviorism, and of operant conditioning particularly, to the counseling process. It will create discussion, I am sure. I hope that the reader, whatever his persuasion, will commit himself before reading to respect evidence as well as logic and to determine to *learn* something, which means change. The 1960's represent the beginning of a period in which much research will be offered in this connection. This book will prepare you to give thoughtful attention to what will be "revolution" for some, a step in evolution for others.

C. Gilbert Wrenn

PREFACE

The 1965 Cubberley Conference at Stanford University had one primary purpose — to explore more effective ways by which guidance personnel could be of service to the young people in our schools and colleges. A number of innovations in guidance and counseling have been developed in recent years, and the conference was planned to provide an opportunity for interested guidance personnel to observe and discuss these experimental procedures. It was hoped that the conference participants would find some ideas which they might wish to try or adapt in some way to meet the problems in their own work.

The first four papers presented in this book constitute the four major addresses at the conference. The many other events that occurred at the conference are summarized in the Appendix. Nineteen demonstrations of experimental guidance procedures were presented. Informal seminars were conducted by such outstanding leaders as Frank M. Fletcher, Henry Borow, Marjorie Mottishaw Anderson, Dale Burkland and Walter Lauterbach. Planned and unplanned informal discussions among the participants provided the opportunity for sharing views and experiences. The four major speeches were designed to provide the rationale and base for discussion. They provided the framework around which the rest of the conference was built. To provide additional perspective after the conference was concluded, C. Gilbert Wrenn was persuaded to synthesize some of the diverse points of view expressed in the first four papers. His willingness to undertake this difficult task is much appreciated, and the constructive result is presented as the final chapter to this book.

The demonstrations were presented as embryonic procedures still to be developed and improved as the result of further experience and the influx of new ideas. The demonstrations included procedures for encouraging college accomplishment among disadvantaged youth, minimizing classroom learning and discipline problems, developing decision-making ability, modifying the behavior of autistic children, reducing test anxiety, building an environment conducive to school achievement, increasing attentive behavior, encouraging career exploration, improving testwiseness, improving child-rearing techniques, using computers in counseling, increasing the assertive behavior of shy children, and improving study habits. A variety of specific techniques were used in these demonstrations, some of which are mentioned in the papers reported in this book. Some of the procedures have been subjected to rigorous experimental tests; others are in a more preliminary stage of development. No attempt was made to present these procedures as final answers, for indeed no such final answers can yet be presented. The conference may be judged as successful to the degree that its participants returned to their jobs and began to experiment with procedures (not necessarily the ones they observed at the conference) that give promise of increasing their effectiveness in helping their clientele.

Stanford University was fortunate that several other professional organizations served as co-sponsors of the conference. Each co-sponsoring organization designated a member to represent it in the Advisory Planning Committee: John D. Black, California State Psychological Association; Dale C. Burklund, California Counseling and Guidance Association; Jack Danielson, California Association of School Psychologists and Psychometrists; Daniel W. Fullmer and Jane Matson, Western Association of Counselor Educators and Supervisors; Diane Gordon, Northern California Guidance Association; William H. McCreary, State of California Department of Education; Jack Murphy, California Association of School Administrators; and Lawrence H. Stewart, Division of Counseling Psychology of the American Psychological Association. As Director of the conference I am deeply indebted to these persons and organizations for their support and helpful advice. A number of other individuals made substantial contributions as discussion leaders, demonstration leaders, general session chairmen and panel moderators. And of course the longest hours, the hardest work, and the least glory fell to Ronald D. Baker, Administrative

Assistant, and Eleanor Worden, Secretary to the conference, who contributed the effort that held the pieces together.

The opinions expressed in these papers are the opinions of each author alone. Though the various authors are probably in agreement on many of the issues, undoubtedly differences of opinion and allegiance are represented by the views expressed here. Such differences in viewpoint are to be expected and encouraged if we are to consider all of the factors necessary for the improvement of guidance services.

J.D.K.

CONTENTS

■ REVOLUTION IN COUNSELING:

Implications of Behavioral Science

CHAPTER / ONE

Promoting Adaptive Behavior:

NEW ANSWERS TO
FAMILIAR QUESTIONS

• *John D. Krumboltz,*   Stanford University

Counselors and psychologists are in the business of helping people learn how to solve certain kinds of problems more adequately. Some of these problems concern important educational and career decisions, such as: "What college should I attend?"; "What job should I enter?" Some of the problems concern personal, social and emotional difficulties, for example, "How can I save my marriage?"; "How can I overcome these horrible feelings of anxiety, loneliness and depression?"; "How can I learn to stand up for my own rights?"; "How can I get along better with others?"

As a result of consulting a counselor or psychologist a person with problems like these ought to be better able to find solutions. In addition he ought to be able to solve future problems more independently and effectively. In short, the counselor is interested in helping to promote a more adaptive problem-solving kind of behavior.

But how? There are four questions that counselors have traditionally asked themselves as they wrestled with the complex problems of their clients: (1) How should the counselor conceptualize client problems? (2) How should the counselor define client goals? (3) What techniques and procedures will best accomplish the goals? (4) How should the counselor evaluate the success of his work?

These questions are old and familiar. But the answers many of us would give to them differ so much from the answers we would have given just a few years ago that the theme of this conference, "Revolution in Counseling," seems well justified. The degree to which you judge these answers to be revolutionary, of course, will depend to some extent upon your familiarity with previous thought and practice in the field of counseling. I hope that you will consider them with the open-minded thoughtfulness that has characterized our profession. While most of us have a tendency to defend our present practices, we at the same time want to find new and better ways of being of service.

I would like to present my answers to each of these four familiar questions and allow you to judge for yourself, not just whether they are revolutionary, but whether they suggest some possible ways in which counselors and psychologists can be of greater service to their clients.

■ HOW SHOULD COUNSELORS CONCEPTUALIZE CLIENT PROBLEMS?

The way we think about problems determines to a large degree what we will do about them. Therefore, I think it is crucial that we conceptualize human problems in ways that suggest possible steps we can take to help solve them. The traditional ways of conceptualizing problems have made useful contributions, but they are weak in that they do not suggest a sufficient number of effective counselor activities.

Client Problems as Problems in Learning

My answer to the question is that counselors should conceive of client problems as problems in learning. The counselor should think of his job as one in which he helps his client learn more effective ways of solving his own problems. The counselor should think of himself as an aid in the learning process. He should see his job as arranging conditions so that his client will learn more adaptive ways of coping with difficulties.

At first glance, conceptualizing counseling as part of the learning process does not seem particularly revolutionary. Counselors and psychotherapists have talked about the process of counseling as learning for many years. Counselors of many theoretical persuasions would maintain that their techniques are employed as a means of helping the client learn. Several excellent books and articles have been written showing how psychotherapeutic or counseling techniques could be explained in terms of certain learning theories (e.g., Pepinsky and Pepinsky, 1954; Dollard and Miller, 1950; Shoben, 1949). However, these authors have tended to explain in learning theory terms counseling and psychotherapeutic techniques that had already been established. They did not attempt to construct *new* counseling procedures from a knowledge of the learning process. The revolutionary development, in my opinion, is that now new counseling procedures are being developed from our knowledge of the learning process.

Many people consider human behavior problems as learning problems for only certain limited types of behavior, particularly intellectual and physical skills. Let us consider some examples.

Suppose that you observe that Mike appears confused and uncertain and is unable to reply when someone says to him, "Como esta usted, señor?" How are we to conceptualize Mike's inability to reply to a question in Spanish? Would you say that Mike is mentally ill? Would you say that Mike has the capacity to understand the question in Spanish but simply has not yet had a sufficient amount of empathic understanding and unconditional positive regard? Or would you say that Mike has not yet learned to use the Spanish language? If Mike wished to master the Spanish language, we would probably all agree that he should be given certain kinds of educational experiences which would help him learn to respond appropriately in Spanish. Very few of us would claim that he was mentally ill. Very few of us would assert that merely listening to him express his feelings about his inability to speak Spanish and our communicating to him our understanding of his feelings would aid him in speaking it any better. Mike's inability to respond appropriately is clearly due to his lack of appropriate educational experiences, and the solution to the problem, therefore, is in providing appropriate conditions so that the necessary skills can be learned.

I have my difficulties playing golf. My drives all too often slice off and get lost in the woods. How shall we conceptualize this problem? Is it because my state of mental health is not sufficiently sound? Is it because no one provided me with the sufficient amount of empathic understanding when I complained about my inability to hit a drive straight? Or would you say that my difficulty is due to the fact that I simply have not learned how to hit a drive correctly? I presume that most of us would choose that last alternative and would recommend that, if I wish to correct my inappropriate behavior, I allow myself to undergo some appropriate relearning experiences.

Application of the Learning Paradigm to Client Problems. My basic point here is that the same conceptualizations which are useful in explaining the acquisition of intellectual behaviors and the acquisition of physical skill behaviors are equally useful in explaining the acquisition of decision-making behaviors as well as emotional and social behaviors. Suppose Susan is unable to decide which college to attend. Shall we blame her indecision on some disease which is afflicting her mind? Shall we say that she has not been sufficiently understood? Or shall we say that she has not yet learned enough about the alternatives that are facing her and has not yet learned how to make decisions in a wise and rational way? I shall try to make clear why I think it will be far more helpful if we think about her problem as a problem in learning.

And then consider a social problem. Jim is painfully shy and withdrawn. How shall we think about his problem? Would you prefer to say that he has the beginnings of a mental illness? Would you say that no one has ever understood exactly how Jim feels about his problem? Or would you say that Jim has not yet learned the social skills involved in communicating with other people. I shall argue that we will be in a much better position to help Jim if we think of his problem as a problem in learning.

The Disease Paradigm. I shall not go into the difficulties and inconsistencies engendered by thinking about all behavior problems as diseases, though, of course, some problems do have clear organic bases. These difficulties are already well documented by Szasz (1961), Smith (1961), Glasser (1965), and Ullmann and Krasner (1965). The way we think about a problem determines to a large degree what we do about it. If we say, "That boy acts like a bully because he is sick," we refer him to a physician, expect a diagnosis, feed him pills and perhaps send him to a "mental hospital." If we say, "That boy acts like a bully because he has learned to act that way," we look for ways to help him learn more adaptive and effective ways of behaving. We are more likely to refer him to someone who can educate him. An appropriate type of instruction may be the most effective therapy by far.

Understanding — Necessary but not Sufficient. An alternative notion for conceptualizing a client's problems is to conceive of behavior as already present in the client, waiting to be released by a suitably warm, permissive, nonjudgmental counselor. It is as if good behavior has already been bottled up and needs merely to be uncorked. Under this conception of human behavior each person already knows how to behave, and once he comes in contact with a warm empathic counselor who understands his feelings and reflects them back so the client also recognizes his own feelings, then the desirable behavior will be released. Most of us who have taken courses in counseling are very familiar with this point of view.

I must make my position perfectly clear. I do not disagree with the importance of a counselor's understanding. On the contrary, it is essential that the counselor understand the client's problems. Of course he must be empathic and warm. Of course he must hold the client in high regard. Of course he must make it clear that he understands how the client feels. I agree that these conditions are necessary. How else can the counselor find out what is really bothering his client? How else can the client gain that sense of confidence and trust so necessary for an effective working relationship? But I disagree that these conditions are sufficient. More is needed. After the client's problem is clarified and the feelings about it are understood by both client and counselor, the client must still learn how to resolve his difficulty. Understanding alone is not enough. It provides only the beginning step upon which appropriate learning experiences can be arranged.

Advantages of the Learning Paradigm

I think that a number of advantages will immediately accrue to counselors and psychologists as they begin to conceptualize client problems as learning problems.

(1) We already have a great deal of accumulated evidence and thinking about the problems of learning from psychology and educational psychology as Bijou has documented in Chapter Two. There is a theoretical and research base from which we can generate new ideas.

(2) We are immediately integrated with the educational enterprise. No longer are we working at cross purposes with teachers and administrators. All of us are concerned with helping young people to learn. Different ones of us may take responsibility for different aspects of the job, but if we conceive of counseling as a learning process and communicate this to teachers and administrators, the fundamentals for co-operative action are greatly strengthened.

(3) We shall be better able to define our goals so that they can be reached. More about this shortly.

(4) We can concentrate our attention on what should be done to develop more adaptive behavior. We shall be less concerned with mere talk about problems and more concerned about effective action. On the basis of what we know about learning it seems certain that if we merely encourage our clients to talk about their feelings, we shall increase the extent to which they can talk about their feelings; and if we merely encourage our clients to analyze and label past events with psychoanalytic

terminology, we shall increase the extent to which they analyze and label past events with psychoanalytic terminology. On the other hand, if we encourage our clients to engage in constructive problem-solving activities, we shall find that they will be more able to deal effectively with their problems.

(5) We shall expect clients to feel an increased sense of responsibility for their own actions. By making clients aware of the consequences of their own actions and the fact that they can learn effective ways of dealing with their problems, we shall produce a heightened sense of responsibility. This is in contrast to the lack of responsibility implied by the notion that one's behavior is inappropriate because one has an unavoidable illness.

Now, whether or not I have convinced you that it may be helpful to think about counseling problems in terms of learning, let us turn to the second question traditionally asked by counselors.

▣ HOW SHALL COUNSELORS DEFINE CLIENT GOALS?

In the past the general approach to stating counseling goals had two characteristics: (1) the goals were stated as broad generalities; and (2) it was assumed that all the goals were appropriate for every client.

We are all familiar with some of these all-encompassing goals of counseling. Here are some examples: "to fulfill one's full potentialities," "to achieve self-actualization," "to achieve a better understanding of self," and, in all fairness, I should add "to promote adaptive behavior." All of these ways of stating goals suffer from being so global and general that they provide no guidelines for what is to be accomplished.

Let me hasten to make perfectly clear, however, that I am not opposed to these goals. Quite the contrary. I am very much in favor of self-actualization, self-understanding, fulfillment of potential and adaptive behavior just as every politician is in favor of peace, justice and goodwill. However, in order to make such generalities useful they must be translated into specific kinds of behavior appropriate to each client's problems so that everyone concerned with the counseling relationship knows exactly what is to be accomplished.

Goals Stated as Mutually Accepted Changes in Behavior

Thus, my answer to the question is that the goals of counseling must be stated in terms of specific behavior changes desired by each individual client and agreed to by his counselor (Krumboltz, 1966). Three categories of goals can be constructed, each calling for a somewhat different approach by the counselor.

Altering Maladaptive Behavior. Suppose that Mary comes to the counselor and complains that she gets very nervous and uncomfortable whenever she is in a group of three or more persons so that she cannot talk with them at all. With just one other person, she is able to carry on a comfortable conversation, but add the third person and she cannot speak. How can the counselor define the goal in this case? The goal depends upon what the client wishes, first of all, and secondly upon whether the counselor agrees that such an end is desirable. The goal, however, must be stated in terms of a change in behavior by the client. In this case the client wishes to be able to communicate with other human beings when there are more than two people in the group. *The goal, then, is an increase in the frequency with which the client is able to talk when there are three or more people present.* The related goal would be a decrease in the amount of negative affect reported by the client when in groups of three or more. This may not be the client's only problem. It seldom is. But it is one problem, and Bijou has suggested in Chapter Two that we take one problem at a time. The problem can be stated as a behavior change and can be described specifically. The goal can be explicitly agreed to by both the client and the counselor. Both will be working toward the same goal. Both will know when progress toward this goal is being achieved. The goal is clear, unambiguous, open and above board.

Note an additional feature of stating the goals in this way.

The goal is individually tailored to the particular problem of each client. The goal of counseling *in general for all clients* is *not* to increase the frequency of talking in groups of three or more. As a matter of fact with some clients, the goal may be to decrease the amount of talking in groups of three or more! When we can state individual goals for individual clients, we are achieving, in the best sense of the term, dignity of the individual.

Consider another case, the case of George, a young man who has a terrible feeling of loneliness. For him weekends and vacations are the worst times of all. He reports dreadful sensations of being alone. It took every last ounce of courage on his part to approach the counselor and tell him the problem. How might the goal be defined in this case? Again it depends on what the client wishes, but let us assume that in this case George wishes that he were better at making friends so that he could have some companionship. The counselor's understanding of his problem will help to establish the counselor as one of his friends. But this is not sufficient. In the long run, the counselor cannot be his only friend. *The goals, then, are that George initiate contacts with other people, that he learn to communicate with them, and that he decrease his anxiety in the company of other people.* Goals such as these are established at the request of the client, can be agreed to by the counselor, are individually tailored to this one client's problems, and enable progress to be assessed.

Learning the Decision-Making Process. Consider Herb, a young man who has no idea what kind of occupation he would like to enter. Herb definitely wants to prepare himself for some type of occupation but is completely at a loss concerning what it might be and how he might go about deciding. How might the counselor define the objectives in this case? Once again it depends upon the client's request. But here it is obvious that the client does not know how to go about making a wise occupational choice.

The counselor may propose that the client learn how to make decisions of this type by going through the various stages in connection with his own problem. If the client wished to do his, the counselor might then help to define some specific steps which Herb should learn how to do: (1) how to gather feasible alternatives to consider, (2) how to gather relevant information about each alternative, (3) how to estimate his own chances of success in each alternative, (4) how to consider his own values and purposes in relation to various occupations under consideration, (5) how to deliberate and weigh the various values, possible outcomes and facts in relation to each alternative, and (6) how to formulate a tentative plan of action subject to new developments and new opportunities. *The goal, then, is learning to use this sequence of problem-solving steps in the solution of personal, educational and vocational decisions.*

Preventing Problems. There is a third kind of goal which has some intriguing possibilities — the prevention of problems. What could counselors do to prevent misery, suffering, waste and discouragement? How many problems in school are caused by harsh and punitive grading policies? How many marriages are on the rocks because the partners were ill-suited to each other and ignorant of their responsibilities? How many students fail to complete their education because their curriculum was inappropriate and teaching methods were ineffective? How many men and women go through life feeling rejected and unwanted because they never learned to approach other people in a friendly manner? How many children are permanently damaged by the neglect and harmful child-rearing practices used by parents? Here are human problems which are not brought to the counselor until the damage has already been done. These are human problems which society at large implicitly, if not explicitly, wants to have solved. Does the counselor have any responsibility for the prevention of problems such as this? If we do have a responsibility (and I think we do), counselors and psychologists will need to have some policy-making role in the establishment of grading systems, in family life education, and in curricular and extracurricular programs. Most of all counselors and psychologists, as well as educators, will need a soundly based knowledge of the consequences of alternative educational practices.

Now that we have decided that the counselor ought to think

of his problems in learning terms, and now that he is going to state his goals in terms of specific changes in the client's behavior that both he and the client desire, we turn to the third major question.

■ WHAT METHODS AND PROCEDURES WILL BEST ACCOMPLISH THE GOALS?

Four general approaches to the development of new counseling techniques are being derived from our current knowledge of the learning process.

Operant Learning

The first approach is derived from our knowledge of operant learning. The application to counseling is that the timing of reinforcement can be useful in producing the kind of behavior desired by the client. We are all familiar with the psychological studies in which rats learn to turn either to the left or to the right as a result of finding pellets of food at one spot or the other. For the rat these pellets of food are reinforcers. If they receive these reinforcers after turning right, it is more likely that they will turn right in the future. We human beings are also affected by the reinforcers we receive, and we learn to do those things which produce certain kinds of desirable conditions for us. For example, we engage in certain kinds of occupational activity because we receive money as well as other benefits for so doing. Money is a reinforcer. Students write certain kinds of papers in school because teachers give *A* grades to people who write these kinds of papers. *A* grades are another kind of reinforcer. Most of us find that the attention and approval of our friends, neighbors and associates have reinforcing consequences. And so it seems quite likely that the attention and approval of a counselor might have reinforcing effects for a client, especially if the client feels that the counselor understands his problem and can do something to help.

Nature of Client's Talk Affected by Counselor Reinforcement. The evidence from several studies confirms that the counselor's attention and approval following certain kinds of responses makes a big difference in the kinds of responses the client makes in the future (Krumboltz and Schroeder, 1965; Krumboltz and Thoresen, 1964; Ryan and Krumboltz, 1964). Consider an illustration. Suppose the client says, "I feel all confused by this business of trying to decide about my future plans. I don't know where to begin." Notice that there are two elements in the client's statement: (a) his feelings of confusion, and (b) his not knowing where to begin. Suppose the counselor responds by saying, "You feel all confused by this business." The counselor is then giving his attention, and thus reinforcing, the client's talk about his feelings of confusion. We would expect from our knowledge of learning theory that the client would continue to talk more about his feelings of confusion. Suppose the counselor replied, instead, "You feel you want to know where to begin." He would then be reinforcing talk about where to begin and we might therefore expect more of this talk from the client in the future.

The kind of response made by the counselor will determine to some extent the direction that the client will take in the future. Counselors reinforce by their attention, interest and approval certain kinds of client responses. By their inattention, lack of interest and failure to respond, they extinguish or diminish the tendency of the client to talk about certain other things. The counselor is reinforcing some kind of response or failing to reinforce some other kind of response whether he knows it or not.

The problem for counselors is to decide on the timing of their reinforcements. The reinforcements should be arranged to promote the objectives desired by the client. If the client wants to learn how to make wise vocational decisions, then it might be more important for him to start talking about where to begin than to continue to wallow around in his own feelings of confusion.

Importance of Reinforcements Outside the Interview. But the reinforcements that occur during a brief counseling interview are of only minor importance compared to the reinforcements which occur constantly outside. Thus the school counselor must have the cooperation of teachers, administrators, parents and others if he is to help some of his clients.

Take the problem of underachievement, one of the most common school difficulties. This problem is produced in a youngster when his efforts to master school tasks are not reinforced. Since by definition only half the class can be above average, some youngsters are constantly receiving low grades. This is the result of grading systems which compare each child's present achievement with the group's achievement rather than with the child's own past achievement. If each child could be reinforced for showing improvement over his own past performance, we could predict a marked increase in achieving behavior. To bring this about teachers, parents and administrators must be prepared to reinforce any improvement in a child's school work no matter how much it may still deviate from what they consider ideal. Counselors and psychologists who understand the importance of well timed reinforcement can help to arrange more encouraging consequences when underachievers start to show some effort in the right direction.

One of the revolutionary developments in counseling is the awareness that the counselor can reinforce or fail to reinforce either at appropriate or inappropriate times. He cannot avoid the responsibility which this brings to him. Thus, the question is not whether the counselor should or should not use reinforcement — the question is how the counselor can time his use of reinforcement in the best interests of his client.

Imitative Learning

A second approach in generating new procedures comes from our knowledge of imitative learning. The application to counseling is that the counselor can arrange for the client to observe *models* of the more adaptive behavior. Sometimes the client has so little idea of what might be more appropriate modes of behavior that he does not engage in any kind of talk or other behavior which constitutes even the beginning of a behavior to be reinforced. The work of Albert Bandura and his colleagues has contributed substantially to our knowledge of the conditions under which the observation of models is effective in changing behavior (e.g., Bandura and McDonald, 1963; Bandura, Ross and Ross, 1963; Bandura and Walters, 1963). A good deal of evidence has also been accumulated to show that the counselor's use of models may influence the behavior of a client. How can this be done?

One way is to present tape recordings of people who are successfully engaged in appropriate problem-solving activities. One effective model consisted of a 15-minute tape recording of a high school boy who was engaged in seeking information relevant to his educational and vocational plans (Krumboltz and Schroeder, 1965; Krumboltz and Thoresen, 1964). Another model tape contributed substantially to helping high school students to make better use of their unscheduled time (Smith, 1965). Other media are also appropriate. The use of programed instruction and other forms of written material has been shown to be effective (Bruner, 1965). Video taped television presentations and movies may well be effective if appropriately designed (Krumboltz, Varenhorst, and Thoresen, in press). Well chosen books may have a marked influence as models. Autobiographies, biographies and appropriate fiction may be selected or developed in an effort to provide appropriate models for the kind of behavior a particular client may desire (Young, 1963).

Cognitive Learning

A third general approach to new procedures, though not distinct from the others, is related to developments in cognitive learning. Sometimes people ask, "If the client is clear on what he wants to do, why mess around with reinforcement and models? Why not just *tell* him to do it?" There are times when appropriate verbal instructions may be most helpful. Although simply telling a client some needed information has very little appeal to theoreticians and others who write about counseling, its usefulness should not be overlooked.

Making Behavior Contracts. One particularly intriguing way of incorporating verbal instructions into the counseling or psychotherapeutic process consists of making contracts between the counselor and client (Sultzer, 1962). Keirsey (1965) has described the use of the "behavior contract" in the case of aggressive, destructive or disruptive acts by children in school. A contract is prepared and signed by each party who agrees to play a certain role for a certain period of time. The child agrees that any disruptive act on his part will immediately result in his being asked to leave school. The teacher agrees to signal the child to leave the classroom whenever the child makes a disruptive act. The principal agrees to enforce the agreement even if it entails carrying the child out of class. The parent agrees to avoid conversation with the child about school and to avoid punishing or scolding the child for being sent home. The psychologist negotiates the contract and agrees to be available for counsel. The beauty of this system from my point of view is that the behavior desired by the child is explicitly stated; the contingencies of reinforcement are known in advance to all parties; and when the child does act properly, he gets full credit for his improved behavior.

Keirsey described other variations of the contract approach. For example, for reluctant learners, it is agreed that when the child is in seat number one, he is part of the class and is given instruction just as the other students are; but when he is in seat number two, he is not part of the class and is given no instruction whatsoever. As long as the child upholds his end of the agreement, he may elect to sit in either seat. If he violates the agreement by refusing to work when he is in seat number one, he is banished to seat number two for the rest of the day. The agreement must be written down and countersigned by the teacher, the principal, the student and the student's parents. Many variations are possible. Keirsey stated that the essential contract is, "in return for getting off the kid's back, the adults are assured in writing by the student that he will take over the responsibility for educating himself and that whatever events ensue must be credited to him and not to them . . ." (p. 12).

Role-Playing. Clients may be instructed to play new roles for certain periods of time. Role-playing is another way of presenting models and of allowing the client to practice and be reinforced for good approximations to the desired behavior. In my own counseling I find that role-playing is a very effective way of getting a client to practice a task under low-stress conditions. For example, a young man who was so timid that he was afraid to return an unsatisfactory article to a store and complain about it, though this was exactly what he wanted to do, was encouraged to practice the act while I played the role of the store manager. A couple of role-playing sessions were sufficient to enable him to return the article to the store and get his money refunded. The fact that he was successful in this venture was reinforcing to him, and he generalized the experience to strengthen his assertive responses in other encounters of a like nature.

Role-playing need not be confined to the interview situation. Indeed, the only purpose of any of these techniques is to set in motion the process of getting the client to learn a more appropriate role outside the interview. Keirsey has described a technique called the "role-shift," which involves persuading the client to try out a new pattern of behavior just so that some information about it can be gained. Keirsey described the case of the child who had maneuvered his mother into the position of having to nag at him continuously in the morning to get him out of bed, dressed, fed and off to school. Clearly, the roles that the two people were playing were unsatisfactory. Keirsey believed that it would be important for the mother to try out almost any other kind of role in order to break the pattern. The first he tried was to have her play the role of the helpless bystander. Her task was simply to do practically nothing. This included saying practically nothing to the child who was dawdling, not eating his breakfast or not dressing himself. Occasionally the mother might say, "Is there anything that I can do to help you?", and then simply walk away. Her task in short was to NOT be very helpful to the child. For several days the child ". . . bumbles around and is late to school or doesn't even get to school, in which case the mother is to just helplessly stand by without trying to do much of anything. Eventually, the child takes over and gets himself to school without further ploys" (p. 7).

Sometimes it is difficult to persuade a client to take on a

new role. Keirsey suggested that the counselor or psychologist can obtain more cooperation by asking clients to try out these roles in order to permit the counselor or psychologist to gain more diagnostic information. Of course this is exactly the purpose — to gain some information regarding how well an alternative role might work in solving the client's problem. If the new role does work, the client is immediately reinforced by the more positive reactions of people around him. If it does not work, a different role can be tried.

Timing Cues. Still another application from cognitive learning concerns the timing of cues. A study demonstrating the importance of cueing in improving study habits has been reported by Ryan (1965).

Telling a person what to do may sometimes be effective, but the timing of the remark is often crucial and the importance of this timing is often overlooked. One parent I know consulted a psychologist about how her children were driving her crazy because they constantly forgot to do the things she asked of them. One of the most annoying habits the children had was to run in or out of the house without closing the door. The difficulty was that the mother reminded the children to close the door after they had already passed it. The psychologist pointed out that the most effective cues are those that occur just prior to the behavior, not those that occur afterwards. The mother was told to observe her children and as they approached the door to give the reminder: "Close the door." Just a few days of extra-attentiveness on the part of the mother enabled her to give the reminders to each child just prior to touching the door so that soon thereafter the child needed no further reminders. (One of my graduate students said it would have been easier to put a spring on the door!)

Emotional Learning

The fourth general approach is derived from the classical conditioning paradigm. The application to counseling is that unpleasant emotional reactions can be systematically reduced by pairing the eliciting stimuli with more pleasant stimuli. The work of Wolpe (1958) and Lazarus (1961) illustrates this approach. Clients with severe feelings of anxiety are relaxed and then the stimuli which cause their anxieties are presented in a gradually increasing fashion while the client remains relaxed. It is a form of "innoculating against stress" by presenting small portions of the stressful situation while the client remains in a state of relaxation.

Obviously, some of the most effective treatment procedures would not rely on any one of these four general approaches that I have described. Some techniques incorporate combinations of reinforcement, the use of models, cognitive learning and the systematic reduction of fears or anxieties.

Now that we have adopted a learning model, specified some behavior changes in concrete language and described four general kinds of useful techniques derived from our knowledge of learning, let us turn to the fourth and final question.

■ HOW SHOULD THE COUNSELOR EVALUATE THE SUCCESS OF HIS WORK?

Thomas Huxley once said, ". . . new truths . . . begin as heresies and . . . end as superstitions." The new truths about effective counseling procedures may begin as heresies, but a rigorous evaluation will prevent their ending as superstitions.

Inadequate Evidence for Traditional Practices

Most of the counseling and psychotherapeutic procedures currently in use have virtually no research base for their existence. The research that does exist generally shows the techniques to have no measurable effect. The few effects that are shown are usually trivial. Of course there are many difficulties with performing adequate experimental studies with complex human behavior, but it is quite clear that we do not already know the most effective ways of helping people.

For example, Gonyea's study (1964), which won a research award from the American Personnel and Guidance Association in 1965, showed that there was a negative relationship between the extent to which counselors developed the "ideal therapeutic relationship" and the degree to which their clients reported themselves to be improved. The correlation was a −.14, not significantly different from zero, but in the direction that those counselors who were most "ideal" produced the least improvement in clients. Certainly evidence such as this should cause us to hesitate before preaching that we already know what the ideal therapeutic relationship is.

One of the primary difficulties in our profession at the present time is that dogmatic statements about the nature and conditions of ideal counseling relationships are made without adequate evidence. We are faced with the fact that outstanding leaders in the field give lists of a few conditions they believe necessary for personality change to occur and then assert "no other conditions are necessary." Consider what statements like this mean. They mean that the search for new and more effective procedures is over. They imply that all the necessary and sufficient conditions of counseling have already been discovered and validated, and there is nothing for the rest of us to do but follow them. I hope you will agree that all the ideas for improving counseling have *not* already been devised and that there are still a few new ideas that ought at least to be tried before we consign them to the scrap heap.

Experimental Evaluation of Specific Procedures for Specific Goals

My answer, then, to the question on how we should evaluate our work is this: counselors must conduct careful experimental studies to determine which kinds of procedures work best to accomplish which objectives with which kinds of clients. This suggestion is revolutionary only in that precise experimental studies are rare in counseling. The few well designed experimental studies that have been conducted attempted to evaluate counseling or guidance services as a whole (e.g., Volsky, Magoon, Norman and Hoyt, 1965). They have asked in essence: "Is counseling any good?"; "Are guidance services valuable?"

I suggest to you that counseling in its totality cannot be evaluated. It is as foolish to say that counseling is or is not effective as it is to say that medicine is or is not effective. It is useless to evaluate counseling as compared with no counseling unless we specify the kind of problem, the direction of change desired by the client, the precise counseling procedure used and the circumstances under which counseling occurred. What we need to know is which procedures and techniques, when used to accomplish which kinds of behavior change, are most effective with what kind of clients when applied by what kind of counselors.

A useful approach is to compare alternative methods of helping people to solve the same kind of problems. The previously cited study by Krumboltz and Thoresen (1964) provides an example. High school students with problems of career indecision were randomly assigned to counselors who used various procedures designed to encourage them to explore possible alternatives and relevant information. For some of the students the counselors used verbal reinforcement, encouraging them to explore further possibilities. Some of the students received, in addition, tape-recorded interviews so that they could hear how other students had explored similar problems. Still other students were assigned to various kinds of control groups so that there would be a basis for comparing the effects of the experimental procedures. Not only were all of these procedures tried in individual counseling interviews, but they were also tried in small groups. The experiment revealed that the use of models and the reinforcement counseling produced significantly more exploratory information-seeking activity on the part of students than did the control group procedures. We found that the model was particularly useful for the male students (probably because the model used was a male student discussing typical male concerns). And although we found no significant differences on the average between group and individual counseling, we did find significant interactions indicating that some counselors were better at group counseling, whereas other counselors were more effective working with individuals.

Studies such as this raise more questions than they answer,

but if we continue to test our new ideas, we shall gradually accumulate some reliable knowledge about which kinds of procedures will work best for which purposes under what kinds of circumstances.

A variety of experimental counseling procedures are currently being developed. Some of them have already been subjected to rigorous experimental tests. Others are undergoing experimental testing, and still others are hunches that may or may not work. The procedures do not constitute final answers or proven techniques. Most of them are in the very beginning stages of development, but they do represent some new possibilities. Perhaps they will not work out satisfactorily in their present state. Perhaps other persons will have ideas of ways in which the procedures can be improved and made more effective.

■ CONCLUSION

I am sure that each one of us as a counselor, psychologist, teacher or administrator wants to find more effective ways of helping the young people who come in contact with us. Additional readings which expand some of the notions expressed here include Krasner and Ullmann (1965), Krumboltz (1964, 1965, 1966), Michael and Meyerson (1962), and Ullmann and Krasner (1965).

I have tried to show that a useful way of thinking about the problem would be to see ourselves as helpers in the learning process. Though we might be guided by some general goals, we would work to specify the precise kinds of behavior change desired by our clients as well as ourselves. I have tried to show that developments in our knowledge about the learning process might be fruitful in suggesting techniques and procedures useful in helping clients learn to accomplish more adaptive kinds of behavior. And finally I have emphasized that whatever techniques and procedures we derive must be experimentally tested to determine their possible usefulness.

In closing, the words of Franklin Delano Roosevelt, uttered at another time in the face of other problems, seem pertinent now to counselors and psychologists: "The country needs ... bold persistent experimentation. It is common sense to take a method and try it. If it fails, admit it frankly and try another. But above all, try something."

REFERENCES

Bandura, A., and F. J. McDonald. "Influence of Social Reinforcement and the Behavior of Models in Shaping Children's Moral Judgments." *J. abnorm. soc. Psychol.*, 1963, 67, 274-281.

Bandura, A., Dorothea Ross and Sheila A. Ross. "A Comparative Test of the Status of Envy, Social Power, and Secondary Reinforcement Theories of Identificatory Learning." *J. abnorm. soc. Psychol.*, 1963, 67, 527-534.

Bandura, A., and R. H. Walters. *Social Learning and Personality Development*. New York: Holt, Rinehart & Winston, Inc., 1963.

Bruner, Fern. "The Effect of Programed Instruction on Information-Seeking Behavior in Tenth Grade Students." Unpublished doctoral dissertation, Stanford University, 1965.

Dollard, J., and N. E. Miller. *Personality and Psychotherapy*. New York: McGraw-Hill Book Co., Inc., 1950.

Glasser, W. *Reality Therapy*. New York: Harper & Row, Publishers, 1965.

Gonyea, G. "The Ideal Therapeutic Relationship and Counseling Outcome." *J. clin. Psychol.*, 1964, 19, 481-487.

Keirsey, D. W. "Transactional Casework: A Technology for Inducing Behavior Change." Paper presented at the Annual Convention of the California Association of School Psychologists and Psychometrists, San Francisco, 1965 (mimeo., 24 pp.).

Krasner, L., and L. P. Ullmann. *Research in Behavior Modification*. New York: Holt, Rinehart & Winston, Inc., 1965.

Krumboltz, J. D. "Parable of the Good Counselor." *Personnel guid. J.*, 1964, 43, 118-124.

Krumboltz, J. D. "Behavioral Counseling: Rationale and Research." *Personnel guid. J.*, 1965, 44, 383-387.

Krumboltz, J. D. "Behavioral Goals for Counseling." *J. counsel. Psychol.*, 1966, 13, 153-159.

Krumboltz, J. D., and W. W. Schroeder. "Promoting Career Exploration through Reinforcement." *Personnel guid. J.*, 1965, 44, 19-26.

Krumboltz, J. D., and C. E. Thoresen. "The Effect of Behavioral Counseling in Group and Individual Settings on Information-Seeking Behavior." *J. counsel. Psychol.*, 1964, 11, 324-333.

Krumboltz, J. D., Barbara B. Varenhorst, and C. E. Thoresen. "Non-Verbal Factors in the Effectiveness of Models in Counseling." *J. counsel. Psychol.*, in press.

Lazarus, A. A. "Group Therapy of Phobic Disorders by Systematic Desensitization." *J. abnorm. soc. Psychol.*, 1961, 63, 504-510.

Michael, J., and L. Meyerson. "A Behavioral Approach to Counseling and Guidance." *Harvard educ. Rev.*, 1962, 32, 382-402.

Pepinsky, H. B., and Pauline N. Pepinsky. *Counseling Theory and Practice.* New York: The Ronald Press Company, 1954.

Ryan, T. Antoinette. "Influence of Different Cueing Procedures on Counseling Effectiveness." *Proceedings of the 73rd Annual Convention of the American Psychological Association.* Washington, D.C.: American Psychological Association, 1965. Pp. 351-352.

Ryan, T. Antoinette, and J. D. Krumboltz. "Effect of Planned Reinforcement Counseling on Client Decision-Making Behavior." *J. counsel. Psychol.*, 1964, 11, 315-323.

Shoben, E. J. "Psychotherapy as a Problem in Learning Theory." *Psychol. Bull.*, 1949, 46, 366-392.

Smith, J. E. "Encouraging Students to Utilize their Unscheduled Time More Effectively through Reinforcement and Model Counseling." Unpublished doctoral dissertation, Stanford University, 1965.

Smith, M. B. " 'Mental Health' Reconsidered: A Special Case of the Problems of Values in Psychology." *Amer. Psychologist,* 1961, 16, 299-306.

Sultzer, E. "Reinforcement and the Therapeutic Contract." *J. counsel. Psychol.*, 1962, 9, 271-276.

Szasz, T. S. *The Myth of Mental Illness.* New York: Paul B. Hoeber, Inc., 1961.

Ullmann, L. P., and L. Krasner. "Introduction," in L. P. Ullmann and L. Krasner (Eds.), *Case Studies in Behavior Modification.* New York: Holt, Rinehart & Winston, Inc., 1965.

Volsky, T., Jr., T. M. Magoon, W. T. Norman, and D. P. Hoyt. *The Outcomes of Counseling and Psychotherapy.* Minneapolis: University of Minnesota Press, 1965.

Wolpe, J. *Psychotherapy by Reciprocal Inhibition.* Stanford, Calif.: Stanford University Press, 1958.

Young, Olive S. "Literary Materials as Aids in Group Guidance." Unpublished Master of Arts thesis, Chico State College, Chico, Calif., 1963.

CHAPTER / TWO

Implications of Behavioral Science for Counseling and Guidance[1]

• *Sidney W. Bijou,* University of Illinois[2]

The implications of behavioral science for counseling and guidance that I shall discuss in this paper are based in the broad sense upon findings from the experimental psychology laboratory and in the narrow sense upon recent experimental studies of young children. I shall, in fact, be looking at research on the "little ones" to learn something about how to deal with the "big ones." In the absence of pertinent behavioral counseling data on the "big ones" we will have to settle for this strategy. Such an approach, however, is quite compatible with a developmental point of view.

I plan to (1) give a few introductory statements about the background of a behavioral science approach, (2) point out four implications of behavioral science for counseling and guidance, and (3) indicate two consequences of these implications, one with respect to the role of the counselor and the other to the concept of diagnosis in counseling.

----

1. This formulation has developed in the research supported by Public Health Service grants MH-02232 and MH-01366, from the National Institute of Mental Health.
2. At the University of Washington at the time of the 1965 Cubberley Conference.

■ BACKGROUND

The background of the science of human behavior is formed by the experimental procedures and data from many thousand studies conducted with animals and human beings during the past 60 years or so. I am not referring to all of the experimental studies published during that period, only those concerned with problems of learning and conditioning.

The fact that an elaborate methodology has evolved and a mass of objective data has been collected from a staggering number of experiments does not mean that what has been found will be useful in furthering basic research or in solving practical problems. To serve in both of these respects, such data must be organized into a coherent set of objectively defined concepts and principles — into a theory. Of the outstanding efforts in theory construction, two have particular relevance to the current topic, one by Pavlov (1927, 1928, 1932) and the other by B. F. Skinner (1938, 1953, 1961).

Pavlov's classical conditioning theory has influenced many workers in psychotherapy and the related technologies and is still growing in popularity. This point of view, for example, is represented in the desensitization and reciprocal inhibition procedures of Wolpe (1958), Lazarus and Abramovitz (1962), and Salter (1949).

Skinner's point of view has influenced not only psychotherapy and the related technologies (Krasner and Ullmann, 1965; Ullman and Krasner, 1965) but also educational and training methods in the form of programed instruction (Lumsdaine and Glaser, 1960). Very recently this viewpoint has, in addition, made its way into special education (Bijou, 1965; Birnbrauer, Wolf, Kidder and Tague, 1965), speech correction (Goldiamond, 1965a), rehabilitation (Meyerson, Kerr and Michael, in press), nursery school practice (Harris, Wolf and Baer, 1964), and counseling (Krumboltz, 1964, 1965; Michael and Meyerson, 1962; Goldiamond, 1965b).

Skinner's point of view has also influenced research and

theory in human development (Bijou and Baer, 1961, 1965a). During the past 10 years his concepts and principles have served as a frame of reference for experimental studies of normal and deviant children in the laboratory and in natural settings. Some studies have been concerned with basic problems such as an analysis of discrimination, concept formation, and social reinforcement (Bijou and Baer, 1965b); other investigations have been oriented toward applied problems such as the treatment of severely disturbed children (Wolf, Risley and Mees, 1964).

Even this very brief consideration of the background of behavioral science makes it apparent that implications of a behavioral science approach for counseling ultimately stem from work in experimental laboratories and theories closely tied to experimental data. In contrast, implications of the conventional approaches to counseling emanate from the clinic, and from theories based on clinical observation and research. This is true whether the point of view is client-centered, psychoanalytic, or relationship.

■ IMPLICATIONS

We now turn to a consideration of four implications of a behavioral science approach to counseling.

1. Counseling procedures should be planned to modify the problem behavior presented directly, and in the situation in which it occurs.
2. Counseling procedures should be designed to deal with specific problem behavior, preferably one problem behavior at a time.
3. Counseling procedures should include recording problem behavior in objective terms and on the basis of frequency of occurrence.
4. Counseling procedures should be planned to change behavior in the desired direction in small progressive steps.

Let us consider each of these implications in turn.

Modify Problem Behavior Directly
and in Its Natural Setting

The first implication, that counseling procedures should be planned to modify the problem behavior presented directly, and in the situation in which it occurs, arises from the natural science conception that the most effective way of changing behavior is by changing the environmental circumstances which control it. It would therefore be advantageous from this point of view to observe the problem behavior of concern in its natural setting in order to be able to see its form and frequency of occurrence and to be able to analyze the specific environmental factors which arouse and perpetuate it.

I do not think that anyone will deny that the ultimate goal of counseling is to help the client deal more effectively with his environment, to replace maladjusted behavior with adjusted behavior. It seems clear from an experimental analysis of behavior point of view that one of the most efficient ways of bringing about desired behavioral changes is by directly modifying the circumstances that support them, and one of the most effective ways of maintaining these changes is by arranging an environment that continues to support them.

Illustration of Increasing Sociability. Suppose we were asked to help a four-year-old girl who is described by her mother as a social isolate. We could follow conventional practices, putting the child into play therapy with a qualified therapist and then seeing whether this course of action over a period of months increases her sociability in the nursery school and in the neighborhood. We could also deal with her withdrawn behavior directly *in the nursery school situation* as was done in a study by Allen, Hart, Buell, Harris and Wolf (1964) at the University of Washington.

The subject, Ann, was of above-average intelligence and came from a family in the upper-middle socioeconomic class. After six weeks in the nursery school, which is considered the normal period for adaptation, it was noted that she spent only a small part of the time at school with other children. Most of the time was spent with adults or alone, sometimes in constructive occupation, other times just sitting or standing about. When she was in the company of adults she devoted herself to attracting the teacher's attention with remarks about her collection of rocks, pieces of wood, etc., and by comments about her scratches, bumps, and bruises. Her speech was hesitant and low, and at times she showed tic-like behaviors.

Two trained observers recorded Ann's behavior each morning under the usual conditions of school attendance. They recorded at 10-second intervals, with the exception of snack time, the time the child spent with other children and the time she spent with adults. The data are shown in Figure 1. It will be noted that during the first five-day period, Ann spent

FIGURE 1. Percentage of time a four-year-old girl spent in social interaction during approximately two hours of each morning.

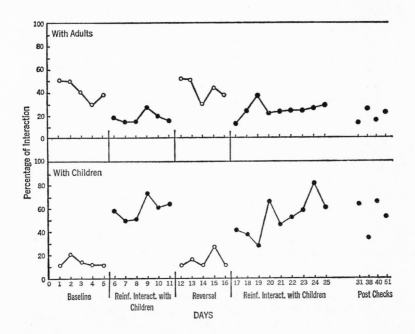

about 10 percent of her time with children, about 40 percent with adults, and the rest of the time by herself.

On the sixth day, one of the teachers was assigned to go to Ann immediately when she observed her with other children and to remain with her and her group as long as Ann stayed with the children. Under these circumstances the teacher watched, commented favorably on Ann's play and especially on the play activity of the group. The teacher was also instructed to give Ann minimal or no attention when she was alone or with adults, including the teacher herself. Under these changed conditions (receiving attention for social behavior, and no attention for isolate or adult-oriented behavior), which were in effect for six days (day 6 to day 11), Ann spent about 60 percent of the mornings in play with her peers and less than 20 percent in contact with adults.

On day 12, and the five succeeding days, the contingencies were reversed. The baseline conditions of dealing with isolate and social behavior were again reinstated. During this period (day 12 to day 16), interactions with children fell to about 20 percent and interactions with adults rose to about 40 percent. On day 17, and during the succeeding eight days, the teacher again reinforced Ann for contact and play with peers. Over this time span, play with children stabilized at about 60 percent and contacts with adults at about 25 percent. Adult attention for interaction with children was gradually made more intermittent, sometimes reinforced and other times not reinforced. The schedule of adult contacts gradually approached normal practice during the last days of this period.

Six days (day 31) after the last day of the study (day 25) the first post-study check was made to see whether the changes persisted. Other checks were made on the 13th, 15th, and 26th days after completion of the main study. These data showed that the changes were being maintained, for Ann was spending about 54 percent of her mornings with children and about 18 percent with adults.

Application to Counseling. I realize that in counseling older children and adults it might be difficult to work directly with the actual problem behavior and in the actual situation in which it occurs. It is possible, therefore, that aids and contrivances would have to be used to get the counselor into or as near as possible to actual interactions. Suppose, for example, that the problem was that the client had never learned how to study effectively. Depending upon the circumstances, several courses of action might be taken. One might be to instruct the client, in specific detail, on how to begin, how and when to move ahead and how to keep useful detailed records that would be discussed in counseling sessions. Another might be to elicit the help of others (teachers, parents, dormitory counselors and the like) who are in a position to observe what is happening in the study situation and to assist (in accordance with instructions) in bringing about the desired changes. Still another course might be to contrive a special study situation in which the counselor would work directly with the client on improving his study routine. This might mean arranging circumstances so that the client studies only under supervision and only in a special laboratory room at certain times of the day. After the desired study behavior has been strengthened under these circumstances, a planned transition would be made to a more convenient setting.

I am sure that there are objections to the implication of working with behavior directly and in the situation in which it occurs. Some may claim that most problems cannot be handled this way. How, for example, could one deal with "feelings of despair" which are likely to occur in many situations? It is true that statements about the "feelings of despair" cannot be treated as suggested here, but some of the concrete problem behaviors which are correlated with or a functional part of these reactions probably can. If these concrete problem behaviors are treated effectively in their actual situations, it is highly probable that the frequency of statements about "feelings of despair" will decrease to a low level or even to zero.

Others may claim that the practice of dealing with problem behavior in its natural setting does not help the client to deal with his other problems. On the basis of the psychological experimental literature, I have every reason to believe that the best way to produce a good problem solver is by giving him training in the techniques of solving problems in specific situations.

Let me point out a contrast here. Many of the conventional approaches in counseling aim to get into and as near as possible to the *presumed* internal processes and conditions of the individual so that *hypothetical* causes may be modified. The behavioral science approach aims to get into and as near as possible to the *actual* situation in which the problem behavior may be modified.

Deal with Specific Problem Behavior

Let us now consider the second implication — concentrating on specific problem behavior, preferably one class of problem behavior at a time. It should be apparent from the study presented on the isolate child that a behavioral science approach favors dealing with one specific problem at a time.

Those who follow this point of view take the position that it is *not* advantageous to try to reorganize, in one fell swoop, the "whole personality" or even to attempt to modify some hypothetical part of the personality such as the "sense of ego-identity." If such global objectives do in fact refer to changes in behavior, then the units selected to be changed are much too large to manage well. If these global objectives do not refer to changes in behavior (and I do not think that they do), then it is not clear how anyone could tell that they had been achieved, nor is it clear what procedures would best serve to accomplish them.

Concentrating on specific problems usually means (1) differentially strengthening behavior already learned, or (2) building new skills. Here are two examples, one to illustrate each type, drawn from research and service studies with nursery school children in a school setting.

Reducing Aggressive Behavior Prior to Treating Fantasy Behavior. The case of Denny, which illustrates differential strengthening of several classes of behavior, pertains to the remedial guidance program given a four-year-old boy in a laboratory nursery school.[3] This youngster was eliminated from a day-care nursery school because he engaged in role-playing (pretending to be someone else) during practically the full school day. It was reported that he refused to respond unless addressed as the character he was portraying, and he refused to play with other children unless they joined him in his role-playing. In addition, he was extremely aggressive toward other children while playing his roles, which were usually those of power figures. (The social worker stated that the child did not appear to know fantasy from reality.) When he did not "get his way," he screamed, cried, and kicked, and sometimes attempted to run away.

The first phase of the program dealt with Denny's aggressive behavior; the second, with his fantasy or role-playing behavior. The procedures introduced in the first phase were continued throughout the second phase. Work on aggressive behavior began with formulating a workable definition of the term "aggressive behavior," which was deemed to be the frequency of occurrence of physical assaults (e.g., biting, kicking, hitting, and pushing), verbal assaults (e.g., "I'm going to kill you"; I'll cut your scalp off"; "I don't like you.") and destructive acts toward the physical surroundings. It was also agreed that cooperative and friendly behavior would be defined in terms of objective instances of following routines and playing. These data gathered by observers over a five-day period showed that Denny engaged in an average of 15 assaultive acts per day. Ninety percent of these acts were directed toward teachers and included most of the categories used in the definition of the term. Experimental changes were introduced on the sixth day of the program and lasted for 19 days. These changes were designed to weaken Denny's aggressive behavior and strengthen his cooperative and friendly behavior. Occurrences of aggressive

----

3. This child was part of a study supported by grant 32-57-0200-1003, from the U. S. Office of Education. The study was entitled "Research in Remedial Guidance of Young Retarded Children with Behavior Problems which Interfere with Academic Learning and Adjustment," and was conducted in 1964-1965 in the Developmental Psychology Laboratory Preschool, Department of Psychology, University of Washington.

behavior brought from the teacher an immediate admonition to stop. If he did not terminate the behavior immediately, he was removed from the school room and placed in the "time-out" room. On the other hand, occurrences of cooperative behavior and friendly contacts were followed by the teacher's speaking to him, smiling, touching him, or offering play materials, equipment, special privileges, or activities. On the second day under this regime, there were only two instances of aggressive behavior as compared with the baseline of about 15. Frequency of aggressive behavior during the next 17 days averaged three per day.

We turn now to the procedures used for dealing with Denny's fantasy behavior. Baseline records consisting of proportion of time spent in personal role-playing and in appropriate play were gathered by the observers over a 19-day period prior to the time the experimental regime was introduced to attenuate aggressive behavior in phase one. During this time Denny was treated according to conventional nursery school practices. Teachers participated in his personal fantasy play, restrained or distracted him when he attempted to hurt others, and gave him attention and sympathy when he seemed to need it.

Personal role-playing or fantasy behavior was defined as verbal statements referring to himself or others as imaginary characters, or actions which carried out a role once it had been verbalized. For example, if Denny made the statement that he was an Indian and carried a drum around, beating it, the time intervals elapsing during the time he was using the drum were counted as fantasy play. (Music periods, which normally included imaginary role-playing, were excluded from the data records.) Appropriate play was defined as playing with toys, materials, or equipment without verbal evidence that he was playing a role.

As is shown in Figure 2, during the first 19 days, which constituted the baseline period, Denny engaged in personal role-playing about 40 percent of the time and in appropriate play about 35 percent of the time.

Experimental conditioning was introduced on the 20th day

and was continued until the end of the term, the 78th day of the study. The teachers now gave attention and praise for every instance of appropriate play activity. They did not pay attention when he engaged in personal role-playing and, of course, did not participate in any of these sequences. It can also be seen in Figure 2 that after the 19-day baseline period, the

FIGURE 2. Percentage of intervals observed of a four-year-old boy in role playing, appropriate play, and aggressive behavior.

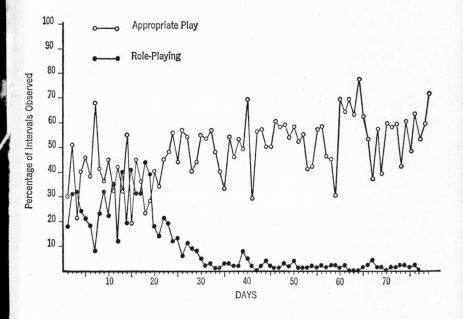

amount of role-playing time gradually decreased and the amount of appropriate play steadily increased. From about the 30th day on, role-playing occurred from 3 to 4 percent of the time and appropriate play about 60 percent.

During the latter part of this study, Denny was also given increasing amounts of guided experience with a normal four-year-old nursery group which met in the same building, and other steps were taken to increase his social skills in preparation for kindergarten the next fall. Part of the program involved working with the parents so that they could help Denny to generalize and maintain the gains he had made in settings outside of the nursery school. This included training the parents to deal with specific incidences and to engage in specific practices according to prescribed principles.

Illustration of Developing Climbing Skills. The case of Mark provides an example of building new skills in a three-year-old boy in a regular nursery school group (Johnston, Kelley, Harris and Wolf, in press). This study was undertaken to see whether a planned program of inducing climbing skills on a piece of outdoor nursery school equipment, a climbing frame, would promote more vigorous physical activity and thereby improve the child's strength, motor coordination, and general social behavior.

When Mark entered the nursery school he was described by teachers as "a tall, lanky boy with a large-boned, spare body, slumping posture, and protruding stomach. His thin arms and shoulders and soft body all give evidence of poor muscle tone. He walks with a shuffling gait and handles himself with jerky awkwardness." ". . . a child who appears well below the social and physical level of the other children. His open-mouthed and staring expression give an impression of dullness." During the first few weeks of school, Mark either ignored or resisted verbal and physical approaches by children and adults. His behavioral repertory seemed limited, including few, if any, skills with materials or equipment, or in play with other children. Much of his behavior during the first half of the school year consisted of random wandering from one activity to another. Occasional attempts to join other children in play were clumsily disruptive and soon made his approach unwelcome to his peers. Information from the family's pediatrician indicated no physical or health problems. The parents reported that he had had little experience in playing outside his home or with other children and few opportunities at home for play activities appropriate to his age and sex.

The method of obtaining data and the experimental strategy were similar to those in the study of Ann, the withdrawn child. Observers obtained the time spent on the climbing frame and other climbing equipment during the outdoor play period for nine days to obtain a baseline record of this activity. As can be seen in Figure 3, Mark spent less than 5 percent of his

FIGURE 3. Percentage of each morning spent by a four-year-old boy in using climbing-frame apparatus and other equipment.

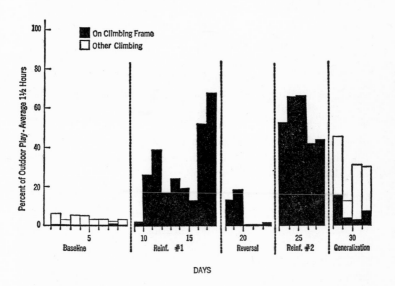

DAYS

time climbing objects. From day 10 to day 18 the situation was changed. A teacher was assigned to give Mark attention when he approached, touched, or climbed on the frame. This period is indicated in Figure 3 as Reinforcement #1. It will be noted that the child's climbing increased steadily and substantially. To see whether there was a reliable relationship between the teacher's giving attention contingent upon frame activity and frequency of Mark's climbing behavior, the baseline condition was reinstituted from day 18 to day 23. The child was given attention for the usual things children do in the nursery, but not particularly for climbing. The percentage of frame activity decreased. This phase of the study is labeled on the graph as Reversal. Reinforcement for activity on the frame was again instituted on day 24 and continued to day 28. Frame-climbing again increased during the block of days designated as Reinforcement #2 on the graph. Now it was important that we determine whether this new behavior would be maintained and would carry over to other play-yard climbing objects. Therefore, the reinforcement procedure was discontinued on day 29 and time was recorded for all equipment-climbing activity from day 29 to day 32, designated as Generalization in the graph. As can be seen, the amount of time spent climbing during the generalization period was considerably greater than during the baseline period.

Relative to changes in Mark's correlated behaviors, the nursery school teachers made these observations: "Mark's vigorous physical activities seem to have visibly improved both his strength and his motor coordination. His posture has straightened and his movements have become much more smooth and precise. His whole bearing has become more 'poised, confident, and purposeful'."

Application to Counseling. In the counseling of individuals older than these nursery school children the necessity of working on specific problems means that someone will have to decide on behavior problem priorities. Depending on your theoretical frame of reference this requirement may or may not pose an issue. It should be pointed out, however, that to rank-order problems on the basis of severity or centrality does not mean that the problems below the top would be neglected but rather that they would, if necessary, be handled successively. It may turn out that after the first one is dealt with some of the others no longer require attention.

One objection to this strategy is that such a procedure deals with symptoms and by-passes basic internal causes. (This objection could also be raised about the suggestion for dealing with the problem behavior directly and in the situation in which it occurs.) Most approaches take into account the fact that during therapy changes in one class of behavior affect changes in other classes of behaviors. For example, psychoanalysts refer to "re-working the material" resulting from lifting repression, and learning theorists refer to "changes in response potencies" resulting from conditioning and extinction operations.

So it is recognized that changes in the strength of one class of behavior may have ramifications with respect to changes in other behaviors. However, if the changes bring about "new" behaviors which we classify as undesirable, we are inclined to say that the procedure produced a symptom substitution and failed to deal with basic internal causes. If the changes bring about "new" behavior which we consider desirable, we are pleasantly surprised.

It might be well to recall another condition that changes with alterations in behavior. When the behavior of a person changes much of the behavior of others toward him also changes. We have heard that as a consequence of a reduction in her child's dominating behavior, a "cold" mother became "warm." We have reports that as a consequence of eliminating a child's persistent and injurious self-scratching, there was a vastly improved marital relationship between the father and mother, primarily because the father no longer found it necessary to use physical punishment on the child. Thus, the question of hypothetical internal causes may become increasingly irrelevant as we identify the relevant external conditions and processes that account for behavior changes.

Record Problem Behavior Objectively and by Frequency of Occurrence

Let us now turn to the third implication — keeping objective records of the frequency of occurrence of the behavior being modified. I am not referring to achievement tests, psychometric measures, rating scales, or class grades. I am referring to the occurrences of responses (or indications of response) selected to define the problem behavior. I am also referring to objective accounts of antecedent and consequent stimulus events that may be related to the occurrences of such responses.

Examples of the record-keeping or data-gathering procedures have been alluded to in the three studies presented. The usual format is to (1) take a frequency count of the class of behavior to obtain a baseline of the frequency of that behavior before an intervention of any kind has occurred, (2) introduce the intervention procedure designed to effect behavior change and (3) see whether the intervention does in fact change the behavior when compared with the baseline performance. For research purposes it would be necessary to reverse the procedure once or twice.

One might ask: Why introduce another set of measures? Why not use the testing measures we now have? The answer to both questions is that we need another set of measures because the ones we have are not suitable for a technology based on an experimental analysis of behavior. We must have the kind of measure that will show almost moment-to-moment changes in the specific behavior under study so that a running account of the course of counseling would be available for continuous assessment. If the records indicated that the recently introduced procedures were effective, they would be continued and extended; if the records showed that they were ineffective, they could be modified immediately. Such records would also automatically give a detailed account of the procedures tried and the outcomes at any time during counseling. In addition, records such as these would contribute to the development of techniques that could be passed on to others in unambiguous terms and could thereby contribute to a technology of counseling. Furthermore, this kind of record system could, with modifications and refinements, be used for both service and research as the studies reported here have shown. Finally, these objective measures could be of value in report writing. They would eliminate the need for giving results in terms of testimony or in terms of changes in weak subordinate behaviors, for example, "He isn't doing any better in his classes but he enjoys coming to the counseling sessions."

A study by Ryan and Krumboltz (1964) provides one example of measuring the process of counseling in terms of the frequency of response. The frequency with which clients made "deliberation-type" responses and "decision-type" responses was shown to be a function of the counselors' reinforcement of each type. Thus, the extent to which clients generalized each approach in future problem-solving situations could be assessed by counting the number of times each type of response occurred.

Change Behavior in Small Progressive Steps

We turn now to the fourth and last implication — planning counseling procedures in order to move toward the desired change in behavior in small, progressive steps. This implication cannot be used effectively unless the other implications are in operation, that is, the counselor should be working on a selected aspect of the problem behavior in or near the situation in which it occurs, and he should be obtaining serviceable records of actual interactions. Since the desired change in behavior can be described in objective terms under these conditions, it would be possible to move toward attaining the objective in small, progressive steps. In other words, the situation would be conducive to programing changes in the conditions that support the problem behavior, deciding which classes of behavior will be weakened, which will be strengthened, with what reinforcers and on what basis.

An example of the use of the technique of moving ahead in small steps was given in the study on climbing behavior. The child was reinforced first for merely approaching the equipment, then for touching it, then for holding on, then for lifting himself off the ground. The same procedure has been used to initiate speech in young children. In these studies, reinforcers are given, typically, first for imitating simple arm movements, then for any sound, then for specific sounds, then for combinations of sounds, and finally for combinations of sounds in the presence of objects and symbols. Working in progressive steps has also been the key procedure in teaching a preschool child how to walk in a coordinated fashion and without excessive falling. Here reinforcers are given first for forward movement on a wide board, then for walking on a narrower board, and then for walking on a still narrower board elevated from the ground.

There are at least two advantages for programing proced-ures in easy, graduated steps. One is that it strengthens small bits of the client's desired behavior in a positive manner and with little frustration and discouragement. The other is that it strengthens small bits of the counselor's behavior — the counselor can see, especially if he uses the recording system suggested, the immediate results of his efforts.

Proceeding in easy, forward steps, and in a positive manner will undoubtedly pose problems for the conventional counselor. These problems might include (1) knowing how to initiate the desired behavior ("priming the behavior"), (2) finding and using effective reinforcers for the particular client and (3) training the "ear" and "eye" to discriminate small changes in behavior that should be reinforced to bring about changes in the desired direction. None of these problems is unsurmount-able if the counselor is willing to become informed in the principles of an experimental analysis and to learn the skills involved in their practical application.

■ TWO CONSEQUENCES OF THE IMPLICATIONS

Now I should like to point out briefly two consequences that might well evolve if and when the implications discussed here are taken into account.

The Counselor as Behavioral Engineer

The first consequence pertains to a possible change in the role of the counselor. Instead of conceiving of the counselor as a reflector of feelings, or an explorer of resources, or a habit changer, or a remediator of self-concepts and values, or a releaser of repressions, we might come to think of him as a behavioral engineer — one whose function it is to arrange and rearrange the environment in order to bring about desired changes in behavior. With this new concept, it will become apparent that the counselor has a most vital stake in the future development of counseling as an educational and therapeutic technology and in the further advancement of its basic science, experimental psychology.

Diagnosis in Terms of Client Performance

The second consequence of these implications concerns the role of diagnosis in counseling. If there is to be an emphasis on finding and using ways and means of effecting and maintaining behavioral changes, there might well be a de-emphasis on diagnostic procedures, especially of the sort that yield information irrelevant to the counseling task. Diagnostic information would be sought only if it could be shown that such data would serve to advance some specific aspect of the counseling process.

It is likely that many of the current diagnostic procedures will have limited value in future practice, not only because they contribute little to the counseling process, but because the results are usually in terms of *traits*. Such results serve well if one is interested in classifying clients. They are meaningless if one is seeking hints, suggestions, and guides for programing effective counseling procedures. The kind of diagnostic test advantageous for these purposes would be one which provided information on *functions* — information regarding what an individual can do and under what specific sets of circumstances. (In the case of a child with a reading difficulty, for example, precise and specific information would be sought on all aspects of his verbal skills and deficits, and probably effective contingencies.) Diagnostic procedures of this sort are just beginning to emerge in the psychotherapies (Ferster, 1965).

■ SUMMARY AND A FORWARD LOOK

By way of a summary let me restate what I believe are four behavioral science implications for counseling. (1) Counseling should attempt to modify behavior directly and in its natural context. (2) Counseling should deal with specific problems, preferably one at time. (3) Counseling should record problem behavior in objective terms by frequency of occurrence. (4) Counseling should attempt to produce the desired behavior change in small, progressive steps and on a positive basis.

Two of the consequences of these implications might well be a change in the role of the counselor and a change in the emphasis on, and character of, diagnostic counseling procedures. The counselor may come to be thought of as a behavioral engineer, and the diagnostic procedure may shift from an analysis of psychological traits to an analysis of psychological functions.

If these implications and their consequences appeal to the counselor, he can advance himself in these new directions (1) by reading the literature on the applications of a behavioral approach to other fields, especially psychotherapy, (2) by obtaining training in the basic and technological subject matter of a behavioral science approach, (3) by trying to apply and evaluating behavioral principles in helping his clients to learn more effective ways of coping with their problem and (4) by supporting research and development in the experimental analysis of behavior.

REFERENCES

Allen, K. Eileen, Betty M. Hart, Joan S. Buell, Florence R. Harris, and M. M. Wolf. "Effects of Social Reinforcement on Isolate Behavior of a Nursery School Child." *Child Develpm.*, 1964, 35, 511-518.

Bijou, S. W. "Application of Operant Principles to the Teaching of Reading, Writing and Arithmetic to Retarded Children." Address given at the Forty-third Annual Council for Exceptional Children Convention, April, 1965, Portland, Oregon.

Bijou, S. W., and D. M. Baer. *Child Development: A Systematic and Empirical Theory.* New York: Appleton-Century-Crofts, Inc., 1961.

Bijou, S. W., and D. M. Baer. "Operant Methods in Child Behavior and Development," in W. K. Honig (Ed.), *Operant Behavior and Psychology.* New York: Appleton-Century-Crofts, Inc., 1965(b).

Bijou, S. W., and D. M. Baer. *Child Development: The Universal Stage of Infancy.* New York: Appleton-Century-Crofts, Inc., 1965(a).

Birnbrauer, J. S., M. M. Wolf, J. D. Kidder, and Cecelia Tague. "Classroom Behavior of Retarded Pupils with Token Reinforcement." *J. exp. child Psychol.*, 1965, 2, 219-235.

Ferster, C. B. "Classification of Behavioral Pathology," in L. Krasner and L. P. Ullmann (Eds.), *Research in Behavior Modification: New Developments and Implications.* New York: Holt, Rinehart & Winston, Inc., 1965.

Goldiamond, I. "Self-Control Procedures in Academic and Marital Problems," in R. E. Ulrich and T. J. Stachnik (Eds.), *The Control of Human Behavior.* Chicago: Scott, Foresman and Company, 1965(b).

Goldiamond, I. "Stuttering and Fluency as Manipulatable Operant Response Classes," in L. Krasner and L. P. Ullmann (Eds.), *Research in Behavior Modification: New Developments and Implications.* New York: Holt, Rinehart & Winston, Inc., 1965(a).

Harris, Florence R., M. M. Wolf, and D. M. Bear. "Effects of Adult Social Reinforcement on Child Behavior." *Young Children*, 1964, 20, 8-17.

Johnston, Margaret S., C. Susan Kelley, Florence R. Harris, and M. M. Wolf. "An Application of Reinforcement Principles to Development of Motor Skills of a Young Child. *Child Develpm.*, in press.

Krasner, L., and L. P. Ullmann (Eds.). *Research in Behavior Modification: New Developments and Implications.* New York: Holt, Rinehart & Winston, Inc., 1965.

Krumboltz, J. D. "Behavioral Counseling: Rationale and Research." *Personnel guid. J.*, 1965, 44, 383-387.

Krumboltz, J. D. "Parable of the Good Counselor." *Personnel guid. J.*, 1964, 43, 118-124.

Lazarus, A. A., and A. Abramovitz. "The Use of 'Emotive Imagery' in the Treatment of Children's Problems." *J. ment. Sci.*, 1962, 108, 191-195.

Lumsdaine, A. A., and R. Glaser. *Teaching Machines and Programmed Learning.* Washington, D.C.: National Education Association, 1960.

Meyerson, L., Nancy Kerr, and J. Michael. "Behavior Modification in Rehabilitation," in S. W. Bijou and D. M. Baer (Eds.), *Readings in the Experimental Analysis of Child Behavior and Development.* New York: Appleton-Century-Crofts, Inc., in press.

Michael, J. and L. Meyerson. "A Behavioral Approach to Counseling and Guidance." *Harvard educ. Rev.*, 1962, 32, 382-402.

Pavlov, I. P. *Conditioned Reflexes*. London: Oxford University Press, 1927.

Pavlov, I. P. *Lectures on Conditioned Reflexes* (W. H. Gantt, Ed.). New York: International Publishers, 1928.

Pavlov, I. P. "Neuroses in Man and Animals." *J. Amer. med. Assoc.*, 1932, 99, 1012-1013.

Ryan, T. Antoinette and J. D. Krumboltz. "Effect of Planned Reinforcement Counseling on Client Decision-Making Behavior." *J. counsel. Psychol.*, 1964, 11, 315-323.

Salter, A. *Conditioned Reflex Therapy*. New York: Farrar, Straus & Co., Inc., 1949; G. P. Putnam's Sons, 1961.

Skinner, B. F. *The Behavior of Organisms*. New York: Appleton-Century-Crofts, Inc., 1938.

Skinner, B. F. *Cumulative Record* (Enlarged Ed.). New York: Appleton-Century-Crofts, Inc., 1961.

Skinner, B. F. *Science and Human Behavior*. New York: The Macmillan Co., 1953.

Ullmann, L. P., and L. Krasner (Eds.). *Case Studies in Behavior Modification*. New York: Holt, Rinehart & Winston, Inc., 1965.

Wolf, M. M., T. R. Risley, and H. L. Mees. "Application of Operant Conditioning Procedures to the Behavior Problems of an Autistic Child." *Behav. Res. Ther.*, 1964, 1, 305-312.

Wolpe, J. *Psychotherapy by Reciprocal Inhibition*. Stanford, Calif.: Stanford University Press, 1958.

CHAPTER / THREE

Personal Worth in Education and Counseling

• *Edward Joseph Shoben, Jr.,* University of Cincinnati[1]

Within the American context — if not, indeed, the world's — there appears to be a common theme running through three of the major revolutions shaking contemporary society. Although it is less than fully articulate, this theme seems to suggest a framework within which the functions of education generally and of guidance in particular can be fruitfully discussed. The theme is nothing less than the old one of the nature and value of persons, but its contours are significantly altered by its determinative setting of sweeping social trends.

■ TRENDS TOWARD PERSONAL WORTH

The trends that are crucially relevant here are (1) urbanization and our dawning and even occasionally anxious awareness of some of the consequences and side-effects of life in the modern city, (2) the powerful thrust toward universalizing the principles of civil rights, and (3) the development of the idea of compensatory education, especially as a part of our

----
1. At Teachers College, Columbia University, at the time of the 1965 Cubberley Conference.

so-called war on poverty. In order to identify the commonalities running through them, each of these movements must be given brief attention.

If we begin with urbanization, it is unnecessary here to catalogue the concerns that have become connected with the metropolitan centers of the 1960's. Crowding and traffic congestion, the pollution of air and water, the ugly sprawl of suburbs and the deterioration of the core city are only too familiar phenomena: and each of them is only too unhappily rich in connotations of inconvenience and downright misery. In response to these problems, however, we are creating a new conception of the city and its historic function. Rather than thinking of the city as a concentration of buildings and traffic arteries within a circumscribed geographical area, and rather than conceiving it as a complex of commercial, professional, and residential enterprises, at least some students of urban affairs and urban development are regarding it as a device for the *civilizing* of human beings.

The metamorphosis of the barbarian into the man of culture as we both ideally and popularly characterize him has typically been a direct product of urbanization. Through the division of labor and the intercourse among men of widely differing concerns that the city makes possible and actively encourages, individuals have found greater interdependence, greater security in their own persons, and the greater individuality that can be obtained only through a broader freedom of choice among one's own potentialities and among the opportunities that the environment presents. That range of choice, abetted by greater control of natural events and a less precarious dependence on daily or seasonal supplies of food and creature necessities, is essentially a function, as Jones (1929), Mumford (1961), and Redfield (1953) have shown, of the degree of urbanization. If the barbarian has been replaced by the peasant, the peasant by the immigrant, and the immigrant by the ethnically excluded and the culturally underprivileged of today, the general model still holds: It is the city to which one must look for the civilizing influences that promise the fullest realization of human dreams.

Nor is this case vitiated at all by the unfortunate fact that the advantages of city life to date have been bought at extremely high cost. The process of civilization very frequently has been (and is) slow, brutal, and filled with squalor and an inhumanity that includes decadence as well as poverty. But this very way of estimating the cost and judging the failures of cities underscores their role as a mechanism for the transformation of persons, for increasing the positive diversity among the socially interdependent individuals that human beings distinctively are. In short, the most vitally emerging ideas about urban problems clearly imply that the touchstone of any action is the extent to which it recognizes the intrinsic worth of *persons* as developing members of a community.

Civil Rights

There is a sense in which the same thing can be said about the increasingly successful press for civil rights. Although the focus of school desegregation, universal access to public facilities, and fair housing practices has been most immediately on Negroes as a group, the basic rationale, mounting in its persuasiveness since the abolition of slavery, has been the simple and incontrovertible one that Negroes as individuals hold membership in the general human club. If they are persons, then their intrinsic worth entitles them to the same privileges and opportunities — the same entree to the civilizing process — accorded other persons. The question of racial differences is beside the point; while differences may facilitate or inhibit one's chances of *capitalizing* on opportunity, they cannot in principle be justified as qualifying one's *access* to opportunity. It is the individual Negro's intrinsic worth as a developing member of a community that undergirds the civil rights movement, not his identity in some sense with his Caucasian counterpart.

Parenthetically, one may properly suspect that a significant segment of the resistance to the extension of civil rights is accounted for by those who reject in fact the notion of intrinsic personal worth, whatever may be their lip-service to it. Such an attitude, given the imperfections of the human spirit, is hardly beyond understanding, especially since it is probable that all of us share it some of the time, falling short in our conduct of our intellectual and moral commitments. For the moment, what we must note about the *de facto* denial of intrinsic personal worth is its cost and its danger.

The cost lies in the fact that the man who denies this normative[2] principle of inherent personal value restricts himself to judging others on instrumental and extrinsic grounds. As a result, he is subject to the discomforts of cognitive dissonance (Festinger, 1962). That is, if he is antipathetic to a class of persons — Negroes, Catholics, or women, for example — and justifies his antipathy on their being inferior in some fashion — more stupid, rigid, emotional, or whatever — then whenever he encounters some members of the class who meet his extrinsic requirement (the bright and responsible Negro or the intellectual and emotionally stable woman), he is torn between his rationalized prejudice and the facts of his direct experience. The result is the anxiety or symptomatic defensiveness that have so often been described in such circumstances.

On the other hand, the danger in consciously or unconsciously denying the principle of personal worth consists in the probability that one who judges others on instrumental grounds will react to others in manipulative ways. In political spheres, the techniques of the demagogue are cogently illustrative. In more personal domains, the Don Juan who regards women as primarily objects of self-aggrandizing conquest and personal pleasure is not unfamiliar, and although the widespread Don Juan syndrome is most cleverly pandered to by such magazines for men as *Playboy* and the ethos that they represent, it is worth mentioning that Don Juans can be of either sex.

----

2. Except for their inappropriate connotations, terms like "moral" or "ideal" could serve as approximate synonyms for "normative," which refers essentially to values or norms. Normative considerations are those concerned more with ends than with means, more with *ought*'s than with *is*'s, more with judgment and evaluation than with description and technology.

Compensatory Education

Against this background, we can move readily to our third social revolution, the extension of the school's services in order to compensate for the underprivileged origins of large numbers of children. We need no longer labor much to perceive the working here of the concept of intrinsic personal worth. The noteworthy element in this move is the authorized and accepted usurpation by one agency of socialization of the traditional preserve of another with hardly an audible demurrer uttered. For the doctrine of compensatory education says, in effect, that the family, one of the few institutions within the American tradition that is regarded with something approaching reverence, is doing a poor job in at least one large region of our society; consequently, in the interest of something more important than the centrality and integrity of the family, the school is to be enlarged to take over some of the family's time-honored functions. Whether formulated in negative or positive terms, that "something more important" leads us back to and italicizes the quiet vitality of the normative principle of personal worth. For example, those who would justify this kind of elevation of the school — which is an arm, after all, of the state — over the family on the ground that it is socially dangerous to do otherwise may properly be asked where the danger resides. Why does the probability of delinquency and crime, unemployability, and low or irresponsible participation in societal affairs warrant this sort of intervention? Ultimately, an appropriate answer that involves more than statements of preference must entail some notion of the right of individuals to go about their business of developing as members of the community without being molested or unduly burdened by the unsocialized violent or the unnecessarily indigent. Conversely, the case for compensatory education can be made on positive grounds: Because the individual's development as a member of the community is our supreme value, when the family fails to provide evidence that it is facilitating this kind of personal growth, society through its schools has an obligation to step in.

Whether rationalized positively or negatively, we have

here something novel in the history of the democratic West. Compensatory education is *not* the same as state intervention in cases of child neglect, cruelty, or desertion, all of which require the presentation of legal proof that the sensibilities of the community as embodied at law have been outraged. Neither is it analogous to attempts to prevent delinquency or encourage citizenship through either public or private ventures like the establishment of parks, neighborhood recreational programs, or youth organizations. Such efforts are essentially voluntary and free from any serious question of encroachment by the state on the domain of the family, whereas compensatory education has a gentle but potent compulsion in it and is aimed directly at correcting conditions which have their roots clearly in the family.

Even more important, it must be remembered that while there is a sense in which the term "culturally underprivileged" is meaningful, the often-used synonym of "culturally deprived" is not. Children of the lower class are socialized in a culture with dynamic but definitive characteristics. The stress placed on the present rather than the future, on immediate gratificaion as opposed to delay, is perhaps central. The greater freedom allowed the expression of aggressive and erotic impulses, the dependence of the individual on such face-to-face groups as the gang (whether criminaloid or otherwise), and distinctive patterns of speech are also definitive.

The point is that compensatory education and all other social programs associated with it strongly imply a rejection of the values in lower class life; and while there are many who have grave doubts about the validity of middle class norms, the fact remains that we are presently mounting a concerted offensive to increase the social mobility of lower class youngsters, accepting with very few sighs of regret the probability of their becoming alienated from their parents in the process. To the extent that this reading of the current scene is accurate, it reflects a normative decision to favor certain values over others, to look upon the family in a lower class context in a different light from the family in the middle class, and through educational means to draw into what is vaguely identified as the main stream of the community a large group of young people even at the expense of sundering relatively intimate relationships formed during their infancy and early childhood.

■ JUSTIFICATIONS FOR CONTROL

And there are few of us who would oppose this trend. The crucial issue here, however, is that of the stance from which such efforts are carried out and the justification under which one group with sufficient power — in this case, the state — determines the destiny of a large fraction of the population, taking over the traditional perquisites of a now weaker agency or institution. A brief examination of illustrative alternatives may clarify the problem.

"Doing Good"

One possible stance — and one that is not at all hard to identify in actuality — is that of "doing good," of philanthropy, charity, or beneficent social action. For present purposes, we may conceive of charity as the making of a gift or grant by one person or institution to another within the existing structure of society, whereas beneficent social action entails making a gift or grant through some alteration of society via a change in its customs or laws. Difficulty arises here, of course, because doing good is not always warmly received. "Do-gooder" is rarely a complimentary term; the plea and thanks for alms more than occasionally thinly mask the beggar's curse, and there is more truth than poetry in C. S. Lewis's comment (1942) about the lady "who lives for others — you can tell the others by their hunted expression."

It seems probable that this ambivalent reaction to doing good has its starting point in differential status and implied obligations. Philanthropy is, after all, the privilege of the comparatively rich, and every gift made is easily perceived as enhancing the status of the giver and demeaning that of the receiver. Similarly, the transfer of a gift to a beneficiary can readily be understood as entailing a debt to be paid in subservience, enforced loyalty, or the fulfillment of the benefactor's special expectations. In other words, doing good flirts dangerously with a failure to recognize the intrinsic personal worth of its object and with a tendency to use its recipients for the aggrandizement of its practitioners.

As it is with private charity, so it is, in general, with at least certain forms of governmental doing good — witness the unpopularity of the dole and the frequent abuses, often exercised with an air of contempt, of such measures as unemployment insurance. Even stronger evidence is provided internationally by Nasser's recommendation that the U.S. sugar-daddy drink the waters of the Dead Sea and by the burning in Indonesia of libraries made available as American "gifts." Domestically, we have found to our sorrow that programs of aid to dependent children have given rise at times to pockets of self-perpetuating poverty in which aided youngsters grow up with unemployment as a way of life and with the sulky expectation of aid for children as a matter of right.

Justification by Might

If doing good is a risky stance, so is imposing the "right" or "proper" procedures or views on others. Studies of authoritarianism [3] have made clear the tenuousness and high costs of social changes brought about by crude dogma and the mailed fist. Domination by terror has a way of breeding resentment, and if there are some under authoritarian persuasion who interiorize the new norms, there are still others who merely comply until the conditions arise which favor disobedience and revolt. In less dramatic terms, the analogue to McClelland's distinction (1961) between achievement behavior motivated by fear of failure and achievement behavior motivated by need-Achievement is worth noting.

But there are more subtle forms of coercion, all carried

---

3. See, for example, Cohen (1964), Hovland, Janis and Kelley (1953), and Sampson (1964).

out in the sincere belief that the ends sought are best for those on whom they are imposed and all relatively free from dependence on fear, punishment, and negative reinforcement. Although he was not the first to catalogue them, Aldous Huxley (1939) was perhaps the most widely attended portrayer of the dystopian visions born of the new techniques for the engineering of consent. Less than 20 years later (1958), reviewing his prophecies made in *Brave New World,* Huxley had cause to be startled by his own accuracy and the rapidity with which his forecasts were being realized. Tranquilizing drugs, centralized control over mass media, highly developed arts of propaganda and advertising, the methods of persuasion lumped under the heading of "brainwashing," hypnopedia, and systematic conditioning all seemed to him to represent the devices by which the authoritarian imposition of human goals and behavioral norms could be easily achieved.

More recently, Herbert Marcuse (1964) has pointed out that the complex and centralized industrial societies of our time operate in part by providing authentic if limited forms of security and a wealth of short-run satisfactions, and by removing the great majority of individuals from the processes of decision-making that most profoundly affect them. Without evil conspiracies and with no identifiable villains, then, the conditions are nevertheless established by which most of us, willingly and to a high degree, participate in the negation of the principle of our personal worth. Staggered by the complexities and technical difficulties in this world of ours, we content ourselves with comfortable and comforting gadgets, protections against the contingencies of illness and old age, and the abundant bread and circuses of affluence — an affluence which is not lessened in its significance by our current awareness of misery-stricken have-nots both within our own society and in societies with which, because of the wonders of contemporary transportation and communication, we must live in increasing intimacy.

Coercion, then, can be cordial as well as brutal, promoted by carrots as well as whips, acquiesced in voluntarily as well as crammed down the throats of the resistant. And there are times when it is clearly essential. If the subway guards at Times

Square during a rush hour were permissive and responsive to individual concerns and preferences, the terminal would rapidly become a murderous shambles. In order to get communal business done, the occasion arises when some single person or agency must make a decision and carry it out; the responsibility of the military commander, who sends thousands of men to death or maiming, is only the most harrowing of the wide range of illustrations available here. The conditions of living everywhere, not just in the technological society that Jacques Ellul (1964) has so penetratingly analyzed, simply require not infrequent instances of coercion; and the history of the old problem of democracy and leadership exemplifies, among other things, the extent to which coercion can become a sought-after desideratum among the masses of men.

■ PERSONS AND THINGS

The critical point is not that coercion is intrinsically evil, unnecessary, or unwanted; rather, it is that coercion entails regarding human beings as instruments, as things to be valued only for what they can be used for. The distinction between persons and things is therefore a central one.[4]

Love Reserved for Persons

Paul Weiss (1960) has suggested that the distinction rests on the fact that, strictly speaking, we can love only persons, not things. True enough, we may refer to a motorist's love of his Ferrari or a statistician's love of his computer, but it is only by virtue of a loose and coarse metaphor that we indulge in such references. The literature of fetishism has much to say about the pathological attachments formed by men for ladies' lingerie, about lonely dowagers who leave fortunes to wet-nosed pomeranians, and about children who weep when separated from a favorite blanket or a talismanic kitten. Such instances of

----

4. It is a pleasure to acknowledge a considerable debt here to Eliseo Vivas (1965).

"love" represent malformations of distinctive human potentialities; and when we discuss a writer's fondness for his battered
typewriter or Lorelei Lee's friendship for diamonds, we are
ordinarily quite undeceived by the figures of speech that we
employ.

Nor need we pause long over William James's old problem
of the perfect mechanical sweetheart, a problem that has taken
on new dimensions in a time when androids, electronic simulation, and self-reproducing machines are so dramatically in
focus. To say that a man loves an android is still either to
engage in rough-and-ready metaphor or to classify him as a fet-
ishist, no matter how exactly the machine simulates the pheno-
types of a sweetheart's behavior. Phenotypically, the simula-
tions of a programed paramour may have high instrumental
value as have many things. But such value is satisfying reflex-
ively and egocentrically; our judgment is directed both to the
things as satisfying and to ourselves as satisfied. But when
we love another *person,* we ascribe a value to him that is independent of our own reflexive need or self-centered wants and
requirements. Otherwise, we are headed for trouble: The
relationships established purely on the basis of one partner's
meeting the inevitably temporally conditioned needs of another
are unlikely to last, whereas the attitude that we call love,
rooted in the perception of the intrinsic (not merely instrumental) worth of the other, is likely to mediate adequate ac-
commodations to the shifting patterns of egocentric demands
and yearnings.

Obviously, one need not deny that this attitude may be
based in the genetics of the human species; and it is almost
certain that it is shaped by the long dependence of human
infants on others of their kind, by the perils of the developmental crises that Erikson (1950) has described, and by the
ways in which the individual has learned to use language to
reflect upon his experience. The fact remains that, given only
reasonable luck in the process of growing up, we respond quite
differently to persons than we do to things. The value of a
person is inherent and is simply acknowledged by us, whereas
although a poem or a pipeful of fine tobacco may also have

intrinsic value, its worth lies fundamentally in its special utility for us. The validity of this distinction is underscored by the rationalization of slavery on the ground that the enslaved were not persons but animals, and by the frequency in primitive languages with which the same word designates both the tribal or local group and mankind in general. Once we have learned to make the distinction between persons and things, we may choose not to categorize all human beings as the former, but the distinction retains its importance and continues to share in the determination of our conduct.

Hatred and Personhood

Similarly, our familiarity with hatred as a human emotion hardly negates the point being made here. Among the meanings associated with the attitude of hatred is the implication of behavior which seeks to minimize or destroy the worth of another person by humiliation, deprecation, assault, or even murder. We cannot, however, aim at the destruction of a man's personhood unless we also acknowledge that he possesses it. Thus, the violence of our hatred is a rough measure of our sense of his intrinsic value. It is for this reason, perhaps, that sheer indifference is usually harder to bear than hatred and that love inevitably involves — and is conceivably even defined by — the complex of evaluations, feelings, and attitudes that we call respect. These propositions hold as much, of course, when the self is the object of respect or hatred as when somebody else is. The peculiar self-consciousness of man is one of those pervasive facts that must not be lost sight of when we consider, as our kind has always done, the riddles of the human condition.

■ WORTH BEYOND UTILITY

One of the implications of our argument so far is that the effort to do good is likely to be most successful when it is perceived as emanating from a respect for the recipient, an acknowledgement of his intrinsic value. Another implication is that some of our most civilized and civilizing norms of behavior are without justification unless they are grounded in the distinction between things and persons. For the hard-boiled positivist, it is technical nonsense to claim that persons have worth apart from their instrumental merits because value is nothing more than the projection onto an object of an organism's need or interest. A cut of beefsteak has value when we have not eaten for a while, but it loses it when our hunger is satiated. In a similar fashion, the value of a man varies with our interest in him or with the conditions which confer upon his presence the power of a reinforcement. A mother has value so long as she is a source of milk and dry diapers; she loses it when we can buy our own groceries, control our own sphincters, and manage our own clothing. If such is the case, then has not the value of a victim for a bully comparable status with the value of a wife for a husband or a friend for a friend? The value may be negative in some sense, but is it not only strong and important but also thoroughly defensible? To the extent that we accept this consequence of the naturalistic position, we find it a little hard to object to the assertions or actions of the Ku Klux Klan or the Nazis. Our previous conditioning may have strengthened an aversion in us for lynchings and a revulsion against the efficiency with which Belsen and Buchenwald were administered, but our aversion and revulsion are merely relativistic preferences for a world in which men are neither hanged nor gassed according to merely ethnic criteria. We can hardly claim any normative superiority for our preferences because, since preferences are the preconditions of normative judgment, one preference cannot on its own be advanced as more desirable than any other.

Such seems to be the outcome of any interpretation of the continuity of man with infrahuman species as evidence of his obedience to only the same general laws to which the lower animals are obedient — of any attitude which implies that persons can be best understood by taking the same position toward them as one takes toward stones and stars and stags — of any view of the universe that holds that value is only the utility, like that of the rain for the grass, that one object may

have for another. It is abundantly clear that interpretations, attitudes, and views of these sorts have produced work that has
immeasurably increased human comfort and extended human
control over the external world. If they have also repealed
man's entitlement to special status, it is simply because that
entitlement is bound up with a religious and metaphysical conception of the way things are that is no longer acceptable.

■ SCIENCE AND HUMAN VALUES

The unacceptability of such a conception, however, is a
function of the fact that science, the regnant motif of modern
culture, finds that ideas about purpose, being, and ultimate value
are both needless and handicapping. Put more properly, one
must say that the functions and contemporary goals of science
are not well served by ideas of these kinds. And indeed they are
not. Nevertheless, it does not follow that because these notions
are irrelevant to science, they are also irrelevant to the norma-
ive issues that confront men. Those who choose to argue such
a case must contend that all knowledge acquired before the
development of science or now outside its boundaries is essentially prescientific knowledge to be improved upon only as the
methods of science are more widely generalized. They must
also contend that the only avenue to knowledge is that defined
by the methods of science. One need not demean those methods, the findings they have produced, or the instruments that
they have generated to point out that such contentions cannot be
proved in any scientific sense and that they represent, at best,
an article of faith that is formally little different from other
articles of faith to which men have pinned their hopes against
the world's complexities and confusions. At the same time,
although it is difficult to overestimate the seriousness of these
limitations on science as the prevailing force in the *Zeitgeist,*
one must also point out that science, including the human
sciences, has put us in much closer touch than ever before with
various forms of truth; and by enlarging our capabilities for
prediction and control, including the prediction and control of

men's behavior, it has greatly increased our power. But power is an instrumental value, and the way it is used must be subjected to normative criticism of the most responsible sort. For example, it is a mistake of the first magnitude to regard the achievements of operant conditioning with human subjects (Skinner, 1953; Skinner, 1963; Krasner and Ullman, 1965; Ullman and Krasner, 1965) as either inherently evil or intellectually wrongheaded; but it is equally a mistake to assume that predictive success or the power of behavioral control somehow reveals the normative ends toward which conduct may properly be directed. The fault is not in our scientific advancement that ours is an age of anxiety; it is in our failure to address ourselves vigorously and imaginatively to ways of coping with valuational problems, a failure which may, in turn, be significantly related to an unwarranted (and, in part, unwitting) extension of the positivistic metaphysics of science into a functional conception of man.

The error here is relatively straightforward. Science works under self-imposed methodological restrictions toward objectives that are more or less clearly specified before actual inquiry is begun. In consequence, it rules out of attention certain aspects of all realms of experience in order to concentrate intensively on others. As a result, any image of man or the world that is sketched on the basis of scientific strategies is necessarily incomplete, and any inferences of its completeness must assume that what is omitted does not exist. Although this assumption is, at the very best, obviously susceptible to challenge, it is easy to understand its being made. The immediate payoff of science has been so large in recent years that anything reasonably proposed in its name has a high credibility. The spread of effect from the positive halo around science's head therefore lends persuasiveness to a *Weltanschauung* founded on only one of man's manifold activities and capabilities. Genuinely potent as it is, the radical empiricism associated with science, especially with the experimental behavioral sciences, is a limited guide to conduct. The engineering of personalities, communities, or civilizations remains open to the most painstaking normative scrutiny.

■ EDUCATION AND PERSONAL WORTH

The applications of these concerns to education, the enterprise currently looked to as the primary means of elevating the downtrodden and underprivileged in America and of establishing new and viable nations abroad, are numerous, provocative, and important. For instance, if we are asked to specify what we mean by teaching — especially *good* teaching or *educative* teaching — we are likely to say that it is not only an activity that facilitates the learning of another person, but that it is carried out in such a way as to respect the learner's personal integrity and his capacity to form independent judgments.[5] This conception has two implications: First, it suggests that teaching is generally goal-oriented, flexibly adaptable in relation to the barriers it encounters and the characteristics of the students with whom it is practiced; it is *not* simply a patterned chain of complex behaviors emitted by people called teachers. Second, it discriminates teaching from such other agencies of behavioral change and facilitators of learning as propaganda, suggestion, and conditioning. These latter certainly aim at modifying behavior, but they entail an explicit avoidance of the learner's exercising his judgment with respect to relevant problems; in short, they involve treating the learner like a thing rather than a person.

From this point of view, effective teaching may include but cannot be defined by the teacher's shaping of a pupil's behavior. True enough, there is obviously no argument against an American child's learning to speak English, perform basic operations with numbers, and behave in accordance with certain customs of dress, manner, and deportment. Equally true, there is no doubt that some impressive accomplishments have been recorded in these areas, often against barriers of diagnosed retardation and low indices of intellective ability, through programmed devices, the manipulation of reinforcement contingencies, and the techniques of conditioning derived from lab-

----

5. The points made here borrow heavily from a brilliant paper by Israel Scheffler (1965).

oratory studies of infrahuman organisms. Without lessening our admiration for these attainments, we may still point out that they give little promise of generalized adaptability or critical innovation on the part of the learner. Under the best of circumstances, the teacher cannot feed into the student's repertoire all that he hopes he will possess as a result of his teaching. Moreover, in those cases where generalization and a flexibility of response to new situations manifest themselves, it is seldom easy, except under tightly controlled conditions that rarely occur in the classroom or guidance office, to demonstrate that the useful adaptiveness of response patterns is somehow generated out of the experiences supplied by the conditioner. Innovation and the easy, self-determined modification of behavior to deal with novel stimuli specify, in this context, a gap between conditioning and its outcome that cannot be adequately filled by simply enlarging the "curriculum," the number of behaviors to be conditioned. That gap is particularly important because it is usually where the teacher's power directly to shape his student's behavior ends that his highest hopes for his genuine education begin.

Even more fundamentally, we may ask whether the connection between obtained results and *only* the reported procedures is as complete as we are asked to believe. Studies of learning under the natural field conditions of even experimental schools often disregard elements of interpersonal relationship and of exposure to discussion and overt, articulate thought that are not part of the specifications of the research design. Practically speaking, this is as it should be. Knowledge is typically deeply imbedded in language and entails a conceptual apparatus that cannot be built up from stimulus-response connections but is imposed upon them. Such an apparatus is partly a product of the general cultural heritage and surround, partly a matter of freely made guesswork and a variable cutting-and-trying among alternatives, and partly a function of motivations, like self-esteem or social approval, that are only tenuously bound up with the learning task at hand. Usable knowledge, in the sense of information that is integrated, patterned, and deployable over a broad range of discriminable situations, entails some mastery of a tradition of reflection, a way of thinking about data as well as remembering them, a technique of selecting responses within one's repertoire that goes beyond simply having them there, keyed to particular stimuli.

In other words, while stimulus-response bonds are surely important components of the process of education, the considerations just reviewed bring us close to the Kantian proposition that the heart of good teaching is the pupil's identification of general principles or the cultivation of a rational consistency both in cognitive activity and in conduct. There are commonalities here with Bruner's (1960) notion of the structure of the disciplines in that both views emphasize a progression toward more widely applicable rules of problem-solving. In the light of our concern here for the intrinsic value of the person, the element to note, however, is that this model of teaching and learning puts a special stress on two matters.

First, the free choice of principles, the commitment to consistency, and the correlative acceptance of adherence to principle against expediency and self-interest, constitute an essential part of human dignity, and the proper goal of social man is to construct a society in which this kind of rational dignity can find full expression. Such a society is international — Kant spoke of "world-citizens" — democratic, and marked by agencies which can rationally adjudicate the inevitable and even desirable conflicts of free and principled men. This fusion of cognitive and normative considerations, by the way, is a noteworthy one. Second, the test of rationality is the learner's growing ability to assess the justifications for any belief or rule that may be in question. It is insufficient for a student merely to have been taught and to give back the reasoned assessments on which his acceptance of a generalization rests. Rather, he must earn the right to confidence in his belief or in his preference for a widely applicable procedure by constructing and evaluating fresh arguments, considering alternatives, and demonstrating a developing power to innovate and to organize new situations in relation to the general rule.

If, like the neobehaviorist view, this one is limited, the character of its restriction is quite different. It errs primarily on the side of being more formalistic and abstract than the messiness and concreteness of the world allow. On the side of the disciplines that compose the curriculum, consistency and commitment to principle, except at very high levels of abstraction, must contend constantly with active changes in the kinds of evidence available, the evolution of new techniques of inquiry, and alterations in the methodological criteria and organizing ideas that creative men continually devise and revise. On the side of conduct and the norms in terms of which it may be evaluated, the dynamics of culture require constant adaptations to shifting ideas of right and wrong and to the impingement on normative judgments of new information and the new theories by which it is interpreted and given meaning. Rationality, therefore, cannot be understood and taught as an abstract ideal to be realized simply through the attainment of general principles; it consists in a comprehension of a number of different and dynamic *traditions* among which as well as within which issues must be settled, however tentatively, by reference to *reason* in the light of *experiences,* some of which may be quite private and yet formatively crucial.

■ PRIVATE EXPERIENCE AND PERSONAL NORMS

The problem of private experience has been a troubling one for psychology, leading to a distrust of the notion of "other minds" and indeed of mind itself, to a sometimes dogmatic insistence that the internal worlds of others (if such internal worlds exist at all) cannot be directly apprehended and therefore need not be taken seriously, and to a frequent exclusion of experiential considerations from our attempts to understand the influences that shape character and facilitate or inhibit the civilizing functions of our corporate life. One position from which to examine the issue entails our thinking of it first from the standpoint of the sources of information a man has about himself and his relationships and, second, from the point of view of individual and interpersonal development.

It seems unarguable that a person knows himself both

from the outside, as he does others, and from within. While other people may not know he has a mind or "self," he inescapably does by virtue of his awareness of his own thoughts, hopes, disappointments, volitional efforts, feelings of guilt or pride, etc. Although he may share the doubts of outsiders about its quality, he is necessarily as convinced as Descartes of the existence of his self and its mental activity. At the same time, through his mirror and many other cues, he knows that he behaves quite similarly to other men. His alternative conclusions are two: Either he is a distinct type of being, the only one to his knowledge endowed with a private self; or other men also have selves or minds as he does, but each has a source of information about himself that no one else has. The second is the far simpler choice to make and is obviously the one made by all of us (except when we are wearing the formal hats that symbolize our membership in scholarly disciplines).

But there is more. Having arrived at such an important inference about his own nature, a person is also aware that he is sometimes touched inwardly by events in ways that are not apparent to others but critically important to himself and that this kind of importance becomes often exceptionally difficult to communicate, to translate from private into public terms. The difficulty of communication can sometimes be relieved by the use of metaphor or the poet's imagery and sometimes by peculiar forms of sensitivity and receptiveness in others; but whether or not communication is achieved, the experience retains its vitality in his internal world. A fictional illustration may be helpful here.

One of the central characters in Rumer Godden's *The Battle of the Villa Fiorita* is Caddie, a little English girl who has come with her brother to Italy to reclaim her mother, who is there in the throes of a tempestuous love affair for which she has left her husband and children. On one occasion, tired, troubled, and confused by having to deal with matters too complex for her childish ken, Caddie is taken to hear *Rigoletto* at La Scala. Caught up in the music, she has the experience of a skin parting, allowing her to stand free and tall, feeling a special unity in things and a goodness in simply being Caddie.

The moment is brief and a little puzzling but clearly memorable. Later, when confronted by the horrifying possibility that her brother has been drowned while sailing in a storm on Lake Como, she is reminded, in the middle of her grief and terror, of that moment at the opera and again has the experience that "it is better to be Caddie and alive — even if you feel half dead."

It seems highly probable that this novelist's example of the inward discovery of meaning — this purely private reassurance that one can somehow deal with life on terms that are not only acceptable but positive — awakens analogous echoes in all of us. Although here is not the place to discuss it, much of what we call our identity hangs on the nature and occurrence of just such experiences, and it seems unlikely that we can fully respect another person — that is, react to him as a person and not a thing — without approximating in some imperfect but significant degree an understanding of his identity, of the way his world is formed within the only partially permeable confines of his own experience. After all, we respond in quite different fashions to quite similar behavior. As children, a scolding reproof from parents who loved us was tolerable and ultimately fortifying, whereas comparable call-downs on the same ground from other people who did not care for us were threatening, frightening, outrageous, and one of the bases on which we learned about injustice and bullying. And we conformed far more willingly to the admonitions of the loving parents than to the commands of the equally right but upsetting adult outside the family. The difference lay, at least in part, in our perception of differential concern and in the differential manifestation in our awareness by the adults of their understanding of our own inward worlds, our developing identities. It is on this foundation that it appears quite legitimate to challenge the efforts of the radical empiricists and behaviorists to "engineer" changes in our personalities or societies without giving some attention to the character of experience and the way it is distinctively organized both within persons and within groups or cultures.

■ WHEN GOALS GO AWRY

But there is another foundation for challenge. The self-reflexive nature of human beings makes it quite possible, as all of us privately know, to respond not only to others but to ourselves as things rather than persons; and to some degree, each of us is as walled off from aspects of his own experience as are others. As a result, we are quite capable of even *asking* that our personhood be violated. We can plead that our education be extended in ways that are irrelevant and unfortunate; and as most of those know who have gone through extensive psychotherapy, we can request clinical help on the basis of motives and stated objectives which are themselves quite self-defeating and, in the light of later wisdom and self-knowledge, part of the conditions which made us feel needful in the first place. The paradigm case is that of the young man whose anxiety about brutality so interferes with his advancement as a Nazi or a Communist that he seeks therapeutic aid to insure his future as a storm-trooper or a commissar, but we need not go so far. What about the would-be Don Juan who complains of impotence unless he feels affection for his partner, and to promote his joy in conquest, wants to get over this embarrassing symptom? Is what is called for a set of techniques to increase his bedtime competence or a reappraisal of his stated goals and their meaning? In the obvious suggestion that the latter is preferable, there is no implication that the case is prejudged or that conventional morality is the final arbiter of such problems. All that is being argued is that the goals themselves are essential foci of educative and therapeutic scrutiny. But this argument cuts in several directions, only some of which may be glanced at here.

Complicity in Confusing Persons and Things

The educator, guidance officer, or clinician — anyone concerned with exercising influence over other human beings — is continually faced with the possibility of complicity in a failure to distinguish between things and persons. Not only is he under the pressure that affects all of us to ignore this distinction at times, sometimes, as we have seen, quite necessarily; but he is also under the temptation to justify his inattention to it on the superficially plausible ground that he is simply meeting a client's need. Requests from clients, however, like those cut from the cloth of our paradigm cases, are troublesome on two counts. One is that they invite the agent of aid to serve as an accomplice in the merely instrumental assessment of human beings. That is, they ask that the therapist strengthen behaviors in the client that deny in other men their intrinsic value. This long after Dachau, we need not argue about our Nazi; and as for our would-be Don Juan, his statement of his own objectives explicitly indicates that he regards his loving another person as a handicap from which he wants to be freed.

Second, these pleas for help reduce the clinician to the status of a thing and define the client-counselor relationship as one of barter. In other words, they ask the professional member of the helping enterprise to function himself as a mere instrument in a technical operation in exchange for a fee, the continuation of his salary, or some form of gratitude for services rendered. If one assumes that this indeed is the way the world works, there is, of course, no real problem. If one takes seriously the importance advanced here of the distinction between things and persons, however, then one may at least intrude the question of how such a relationship affects the experience of the client, the shape of his inward world. One hypothesis is that it serves subtly to promote an implicit view of human interactions as essentially a commercial affair. If a man is clever, he can get much from others at a low price; if he is not sufficiently watchful, he can be outrageously swindled. But whether he is clever or careless, he is only trading what instrumental value he can find or represent in himself for the instrumental value he can somehow evoke from others. It follows that his self-esteem is dependent in some meaningful degree on his judgment of himself as a manipulator and bargainer in the human marketplace.

The Central Role of Purpose
in Education and Counseling

The business of education and of the processes of guidance is less (which is *not* synonymous with "not at all") with the technology of fulfilling client-set goals than with the critical examination of these aims, less with *how's* and more with *what's* and *why's*. One of the hallmarks of an educated man or a successfully helped client is one of the many styles consistent with what Socrates had in mind, in the *Apology,* when he argued that the examined life is the only one worth living. What are common to the styles of the examined life are (a) a proclamation of oneself as responsible for one's own actions, *i.e.,* the acknowledgement of oneself as a selective, choosing being, (b) a growing and developing disposition to inquire critically into the range, nature, and implications of the alternatives one has available and into the character of the motives and incentives involved in one's discarding some to accept others, and (c) perhaps most crucially of all, an ongoing and probably endless quest for touchstones by which to evaluate oneself and one's conduct.

These self-developed standards obviously change with time and experience, and as they change, they influence the process of examination itself. To the extent that the changes yield a greater harvest of self-knowledge, a widened sense of self-determination, and an enlarged capacity to act in accordance with the principle of intrinsic personal value, they represent psychological growth; to the extent that they narrow the experience of inner-directedness, entail increased degrees of self-deception, and blur the distinction between things and persons, they suggest pathology and a failure to realize potential assets that are distinctively human. The engineering of behavioral means, then, while never irrelevant, seems essentially secondary to this normative function of construing ends. The man unskilled in normative judgment and inattentive to its implications for his behavior is likely to be one who defends his goals, as so many of us are so frequently prone to do, on the dubious and self-defeating but often compelling grounds that they are the ones he is equipped to pursue. There are few clearer or more touching illustrations of rationalization, and its consequences are rarely positive or, in any long-range sense, rewarding.

Basic Commitments in School and Clinic

A normative emphasis on goals and a deliberate, intentional effort to facilitate the examined life impose upon the educator and clinician two basic commitments: One is to help his pupil or patient develop his capacities for candid and foresightful self-evaluation but *not* necessarily to determine or give content to his conclusions. His professional focus is on a process rather than a particular outcome and on encouraging the use of a broad set of criteria rather than on any particular pattern of legitimate human objectives that satisfy the criteria. Nevertheless, he also has a second commitment to refuse his aid, particularly his technological or sheerly behavioral-engineering aid, whenever it is demanded in a context that violates the central principle of intrinsic personal worth.

These two commitments, obviously closely related, rest upon three considerations. First, as has already been pointed out, any failure to observe them involves the helper as an accessory in the basic confusion of the helped — a confusion of the reactions that can properly be made to things with those that can properly be made to persons. Second, they are crucial ingredients in a relationship which, through the model it conveys of appropriate and effective ways of coping with human problems, may well be the fundamental agency by which change is achieved, especially change in one's normative perception of the human condition, one's basic orientation toward the world, and one's way of experiencing one's self in relation to others.[6] Finally, such commitments constitute the moral protection that a professional in this risky field needs against becoming a technician whose services are for hire to customers. Although a

---

6. On the general process of modeling, see Bandura and Walters (1963). I have tried elsewhere to consider the role of models in psychotherapy and similar normative contexts (Shoben, 1963a, 1963b, 1965).

technician may practice in accordance with a code of ethics, his abstention from the concerns outlined here implies a loyalty to competence above the civilizing use of competence, a state of affairs that can readily involve him in the marketplace image of human affairs and lead to an analogue of the authentic but limited and socially disruptive honor that Sancho Panza observed among the thieves.

■ INTEGRATING SCIENTIFIC AND NORMATIVE TRADITIONS

To say all this is to say that persons are transitional creatures, eternally creating or discovering horizons beyond their available understandings that have been consensually validated. The inventors of science and its beneficiaries, they are not to be wholly caught in its net. They can be understood — which means that *we* can be understood — only if the principles and techniques of science are coupled with normative ideas. If the result is ambiguity and paradox, the case is far from hopeless. As Aristotle pointed out, the degree of precision in any inquiry must be proportionate to the subject. While ambiguity in mathematics is a mistake, it is not necessarily an error in poetry, and poetry is probably one of the basic devices by which human experience is communicated, shared, and assimilated. As a matter of fact, one of the apparently enduring (and rather reassuring) advantages of Betz cells over computers is that they can deal in some more or less effective fashion with vague but meaningful ideas that would short-circuit a 7090. Were it otherwise — were we without art, speculative thought, and the normative disciplines — we should surely be less than human and quite probably without science.

Similarly, we need not be crippled by the fact that many of our most cherished, most hopeful, and most innovative statements about civilized forms of human interaction are not subject to full verification. We have always known that the truth or falsity of normative assertions cannot be incontrovertibly demonstrated; we now have some idea of why. The normative meanings that each of us extracts from experience are compounded of a variety of perceptions over time, some of which are subliminal in their character. In addition, the process of reflection, through which the perceptions are given manageable form, is itself conditioned in distinctive ways by the unique history of the reflecting individual. Finally, while the play of reflection over experience yields sensed meanings of high and determinative significance, there remains a poignant gulf between these forms of tacit awareness and their translation into words. Our normative ideas, then, are efforts to render in communicable configurations a big, buzzing, booming confusion of perceptions and subceptions, received and organized within the related but different frameworks of both a cultural tradition of which each of us is a part and a developing private world into which each of us is locked, and formulated in the imperfect mechanism of language. It is no wonder that myth and metaphor, misunderstanding and correction, a vital quest without a clearly designated destination, are the trademarks of our normative communication.

But if this state of affairs puts a heavy burden on rationality, the ideal of reason is to follow the evidence wherever it leads and to do the best it can with the twilight zones of experience and thought, especially when those twilight zones are the locus of the recurrent, pressing problems from which civilizations take their point of departure. What we mean by civilizations are those patterns of corporate life that give the widest range to personal development on the basis of a crucial distinction between persons and things.

In an age like our own, when we have learned a great deal about the techniques for engineering behavioral structures and technologizing human relationships, one of the gravest questions before us is that of how to employ our powerful methods, including the new technologies of human learning, in the service of normative wisdom. It is possible that our first and most critical step is that of recognizing the inherently normative nature of the human spirit and insuring ample room for its expression in all aspects of the human enterprise. Nowhere is this concern more vital than in the classroom, the guidance office, and the clinic, the places where the behavioral sciences and our normative traditions necessarily mingle in our explicit search for a safer, more zestful, and more humane world.

REFERENCES

Bandura, A., and R. H. Walters. *Social Learning and Personality Development.* New York: Holt, Rinehart, & Winston, Inc. 1963.

Bruner, J. *The Process of Education.* Cambridge: Harvard University Press, 1960.

Cohen, A. R. *Attitude Change and Social Influence.* New York: Basic Books, Inc., 1964.

Ellul, J. *The Technological Society.* New York: Alfred A. Knopf, Inc., 1965.

Erikson, E. *Childhood and Society.* New York: W. W. Norton & Company, Inc., 1950.

Festinger, L. "Cognitive Dissonance." *Sci. American,* 1962, 207, 93-102.

Hovland, C., I. Janis, and H. Kelley. *Communication and Persuasion.* New Haven: Yale University Press, 1953.

Huxley, A. *Brave New World.* New York: Harper & Row, Publishers, 1942.

Huxley, A. *Brave New World Revisited.* New York: Harper & Row, Publishers, 1958.

Jones, T. J. *Essentials of Civilization.* New York: Holt, Rinehart & Winston, Inc., 1929.

Krasner, L., and L. Ullmann (Eds.). *Research in Behavior Modification.* New York: Holt, Rinehart, & Winston, Inc., 1965.

Lewis, C. S. *The Screwtape Letters.* London: Fontana Books, 1942.

Marcuse, H. *One-dimensional Man.* Boston: Beacon Press, 1964.

McClelland, D. *Personality.* New York: Holt, Rinehart & Winston, Inc., 1951.

Mumford, L. *The City in History.* New York: Harcourt, Brace, & World, Inc., 1961.

Redfield, R. *The Primitive World and Its Transformations.* Ithaca, N. Y.: Cornell University Press, 1961.

Sampson, E. E. (Ed.). *Approaches, Contexts, and Problems of Social Psychology.* Englewood Cliffs, N. J.: Prentice-Hall, Inc. 1964.

Scheffler, I. "Philosophical Models of Teaching." *Harvard educ. Rev.,* 1965, 35, 131-143.

Shoben, E. J., Jr. "The Counseling Experience as Personal Development." *Personnel guid. J.,* 1965, 44, 224-230.

Shoben, E. J., Jr. "Moral Behavior and Moral Learning." *Religious Educ.,* 1963(a), 48, 137-145.

Shoben, E. J., Jr. "The Therapeutic Object: Men or Machines?" *J. counsel. Psychol.,* 1963(b), 10, 264-268.

Skinner, B. F. "Behaviorism at Fifty." *Science,* 1963, 140, 951-958.

Skinner, B. F. *Science and Human Behavior.* New York: The Macmillan Co., 1953.

Ullmann, L., and L. Krasner (Eds.). *Case Studies in Behavior Modification.* New York: Holt, Rinehart, & Winston, Inc., 1965.

Vivas, E. "Things and Persons." *Modern Age,* 1965, 9, 119-131.

Weiss, P. "Love in a Machine Age," in S. Hook (Ed.), *Dimensions of Mind.* New York: New York University Press, 1960, pp. 193-197.

CHAPTER / FOUR

Counseling Perspectives:

OLD AND NEW

• *H. B. McDaniel,* Stanford University

This is a gentle revolution. Its modest claims are almost immodestly proclaimed. It does not ask for unconditional surrender — or even for unconditional positive regard.

There have been no calls to send in the marines or even the shadowy C.I.A.

Yet some good people will see the proposals of this conference as heresy.

As I have drifted through this conference and have listened to the questions raised by the participants, I free-associate the dilemma expressed in a quotation in an otherwise forgotten book on the philosophy of education.

> The Master appeared before his charges and asked,
> "What would you learn of me?" and the reply came,
> "How shall we care for our bodies?
> How shall we rear our children?
> How shall we live with our fellow man?
> For what purposes shall we live?"
> The Master pondered these questions and sorrow was
> in his heart for his learning touched none of them.

Krumboltz and Bijou, in Chapters One and Two, have laid out in clear and concise form the goals and processes of behavioral counseling. The statements of process have been supported by brief and illustrative examples of the research on which the structure is built. The demonstrations have sought to turn spotlights on some of the rather specific hypotheses on which research has yielded data. In some ways I am troubled.[1] Have we presented these explorations into some of the facets of a powerful hypothesis for modifying behavior as an already completed building? Can they not be viewed more honestly as systematic approaches to finding a real problem on which a student needs help and designing and testing a way to help with that specific problem? If we depart from this model of an empirical-inductive approach, then it seems to me that we have lost the essential lesson of this conference: Problems can be solved if we behave as scientists and approach each problem in a spirit of search rather than in a spirit of communicating an answer.

Let me assure you that to the extent of my ability I will treat you as *persons,* not *things.* This conference was designed to deal in an explicative way with the behavioral approach to counseling. We had no conscious interest in converting you, whether by the storm-trooper massive assault, or by the subtle sublimation of other alternatives, to just one way of dealing with your fellow man. We have not sought to achieve complete transference.

I shall seek, then, to communicate the meaning this conference, its ideas and its relationships have for me. My communication is for you to use in finding meanings for yourselves, in your own private ways, and in terms of your values and experience. I am confident that in your own way you will achieve and live the *examined* life.

Shoben's reminder in Chapter Three that counselors need to consider their fundamental view of man is perfectly appropriate. Indeed such examination is the first step in any systematic comparative study of various approaches to the aims and claims of any particular science of man. Ask yourselves, then, whose values you are reinforcing. Is your counseling a subtle form of coercion? Can you accept the responsibilities which doing good for someone else brings? Can you also accept that the possible dangers of such actions do not justify doing nothing?

■ DIMENSIONS OF THE NEW COUNSELOR

Yet consider the courage of the proposals. They ask only to be tried — and evaluated. They make it respectable again to use common sense — to deal directly with what the counselor sees and hears. The top of the iceberg, the visible part, is important. Its movement does indicate the movement of the hidden mass.

To oversimplify, the revolution has overthrown "um-hmm" and "you feel," replacing them with "that's good" and "try this." The counselor not only listens — attentively, empathically — but also talks and does — even thinks and plans.

What the counselor does *outside* of the office — in developing curriculum, in modifying teacher behavior, in building a better learning environment — is important.

To all of these dimensions of the new counselor I give positive reinforcement, a pat on the back — high up.

In the climbing society of the nursery school I want my grandson to climb. I want him to play with other children — even if he does push and shove. I want Mike to reply "Muy bien" when I ask "Como esta usted?" I want Herb to gather facts and use reason in making his decisions.

The counselor of the future will be better able to help young people achieve behaviors like these and many more. The purpose of the proposals made in the preceding speeches has been to suggest new ways of formulating the problems and to propose possibly more effective ways of helping people to engage in the constructive activities that they desire.

▨ EVOLVING CHARACTERISTICS OF BEHAVIORAL COUNSELING

At our opening session Dean Robert Wert stated well the purposes of the Cubberley Conferences: (1) to take a cold, hard look at the status and development of a field, and (2) to generate innovations.

The behavioral approach to counseling is not wholly new.

It makes much use of experience, research, and practices that have been employed for many years. It does represent a number of different emphases, emphases which might be embodied in what Bijou referred to in Chapter Two as a theoretical orientation. As I see it there are four major emphases evident at this time.

Empirical-Inductive Approach to Problems

A shift from a theoretical-deductive approach to an empirical-inductive one is evident in dealing with each client or group of clients. This is the same shift of emphasis which McDonald has urged for those engaged in educational research.[1] In counseling this means that the counselor focuses attention on the goals and behaviors of each client and sets as his task the planning of an experience that can yield satisfaction to the client and at the same time move him in the direction of the goal he has set. This is a change in emphasis. Much of counseling, especially that which falls under the general tent of the psychotherapeutic tradition, has proceeded from a theoretical-deductive approach. The counselor has tended to ask, "What does the basic theory indicate should be done for this client?" In the future he will ask, "On the basis of the facts we know about learning, what procedures seem most likely to help this client learn to engage in the kind of activities that will produce the satisfactions he wants?"

Specification of Behavior

A second notable shift, not unrelated, is a shift from the general to the specific. In behavioral counseling much more attention is paid to what one does, to the specific reinforcement of a specific act rather than just the provision of an all-enveloping warmth. The fact that behavioral counseling has drawn heavily from experiments on animals governs this focus on

----

1. F. J. McDonald, "Research on Learning in School Settings." Paper presented at the Western Regional Conference on Educational Research, San Francisco, January 29, 1965 (mimeo).

specificity in an interesting way. With an animal one has to be much more specific in planning the learning stimulus and in the timing of reinforcement for specific behaviors. The very growth of language itself has tended to entrap the psychotherapist into a love for words and their use even as substitutes for other behavior. In the future counselors will be less likely to ask, "Is his general adjustment enhanced?" and more likely to ask, "How many times did he volunteer in class discussions yesterday?"

Use of Behavioral Science Methods

Counselors have always utilized the behavioral sciences. The current shift is from the use of the product of the behavioral sciences, knowledge, to the use of the methods or processes of behavioral science. This shift from behavioral science knowledge to behavioral science process is evident in the emphasis upon counseling as a learning process and in the emphasis on experimental research procedures. Major developments in the behavioral sciences have contributed to and made possible this new approach. In the future counselors will be less likely to ask, "How have others done it?" and more likely to ask, "Why don't we set up an experiment to see if this new approach is more effective?"

Incompleteness of Procedures and Theory

Behavioral counseling is still groping for a framework in which human problems, effective procedures for their solution, and an adequate theory can be integrated. The pioneering proponents of behavioral counseling have been so busy developing proposals, testing hypotheses and evaluating outcomes that they have not yet had time to fashion the walls from the blocks they have built.

Human behavior is complex. It is this very complexity which has lead personality theorists to the formulation of theoretical constructs which are assumed to have validity yet remain untested, and in many cases untestable, hypotheses. To some extent the development of the behavioral approach to counseling has been inevitable. The change in man's thinking about science, from the perception that science is the impersonal creator of knowledge to the perception that science itself is progress, has value for man's own very personal development. This outcome was foretold many years ago by Will Durant.

But as for us grown-ups — is there any likelihood that we may be able to mold ourselves into something better than we are?

Psychology stands today where physics stood when Francis Bacon wrote his "Advancement of Learning" three hundred years ago. With an audacity that startled even the brave Renaissance, Bacon laid down a program for the sciences, pointed to the vital problems that craved solution, and predicted, on page after page, the conquests that would come with the new knowledge. Today these physical triumphs are real, universal, and profound, far beyond even Bacon's royal imagining; and everywhere physics and chemistry, mathematics and mechanics, have remade the face of the earth nearer to the will of man. Only man himself, his will and his character, seem to have remained unchanged.

. . . .

Synthesis is always more difficult than analysis; psychology has not yet put together the human nature which it has taken apart; and it is still easier to describe man than to say what he should be and how he may be changed. We have touched one aspect of a great subject which in our century will draw many initiative minds. We have the knowledge, now we seek the art, to remake ourselves as we have remade continents and seas, but knowledge is power, and every science becomes an art at last, bringing forth fruits to enlarge the empire of man. Before our children pass away, men will be building minds and hearts as today they build ships and planes. Human impulses, which have remained becalmed and almost changeless while all the world without has been transformed, will be consciously reshaped to the subtle and accelerated life which restless invention makes. Already the mental capacity of man has been increased and multiplied, so that the highest modern mind seems to belong to another species than the slow reactions of the peasant. Some day our brains will catch up with our instruments, our wisdom with our knowledge, our purposes with our powers. Then at last we shall behave like human beings.[2]

----
2. Will Durant, *The Mansions of Philosophy* (New York: Simon and Schuster, Inc., 1929), pp. 255, 278. Copyright © 1929 by Simon and Schuster, Inc.

■ SHIFTING EMPHASES IN COUNSELING AND GUIDANCE

Counseling and guidance has undergone many revolutions and shifts in emphasis during its short history. The one we are talking about today is certainly not the first and, if we can extrapolate from history, certainly will not be the last.

In order to gain some perspective on the topics of concern to counselors in past years as contrasted to the topics discussed at this conference, it might be helpful to note the titles of books, courses and dissertation titles representative of the field in years past. Because of our present location I have chosen to trace the development of these topics here at Stanford University. While there might well be some differences in emphasis at different institutions, let us examine the record at Stanford for the years 1909-1948.

In 1911 Professor Lewis Terman gave a course on *Educational Hygiene.* In 1911 John Wesley Raymer wrote an M.A. thesis: "Advisory Systems in Large High Schools." In 1912 C. L. Jacobs wrote on "Vocational Guidance with Special Reference to the Determination of Aptitude." The first "guidance" course came in 1914 when Professor Bently gave *High Schools Advisers' Course.* At this time Lewis Terman was teaching *Psychology of Exceptional Child, Mental Examination of Children,* and *Psychology of Endowment.* In 1917 *Vocational Guidance in High Schools* by Professor Proctor appeared.

Early Ph.D. theses included the following:

1919	William M. Proctor	"The Use of Psychological Tests in Educational and Vocational Guidance of High School Pupils"
	S. C. Kohs	"Intelligence Measurement: A Psychological and Statistical Study Based Upon the Block-Design Tests"
1920	Arthur Otis	"An Absolute Point Scale for the Group Measurement of Intelligence"

1922	Giles M. Ruch	"The Influence of the Factor of Intelligence on the Form of the Learning Curve"
	Kimball Young	"Mental Differences in Certain Immigrant Groups"
1924	T. W. MacQuarrie	"A Measure of Mechanical Ability"
	Jennie B. Wyman	"Interest Tests of a Group of Gifted Children (On the Influence of Interest on Relative Success)"
1930	David Segel	"Differential Prediction of Ability as Represented by College Subject Groups"
1931	R. G. Bernreuter	"Evaluation of a Proposed New Method for Constructing Personality Traits Tests"
1932	C. Gilbert Wrenn	"Relationship of Intelligence to Certain Interests, Personality Traits, and Vocational Choices of College Students."

In 1932 Stanford held a summer *Conference on Guidance and Personnel* which was described in these words:

Problems of guidance and personnel in junior and senior high school, junior college and higher institutions will be given consideration in a ten-day conference meeting July 5 to July 15. Leadership will be provided by members of the regular staff and by other specialists in guidance and personnel.

In 1936 courses appeared entitled *Home and Community Influence Upon the Personality Development of Children, Principles of Personality Development,* and *Diagnosis and Treatment of Behavior Problems* by Professor Fenton.

The summary of the period 1909-1948 indicates a total of 560 research studies, either directly in or related to the field of guidance. The greatest number, 149, have been in the category, "Characteristics of Students." "Surveys of Guidance" and

"Occupational Studies" are next in order with 126 and 115, respectively. "Appraisal Techniques," with 84 studies reported, was significantly represented. "Counseling Techniques" and "Group Guidance Activities" were seldom topics of interest to the researchers represented during this period, though the current Cubberley Conference may stimulate more interest in these two important areas of guidance work.

Thus, a profession which began as advice-giving, then developed a strong measurement component with emphasis on traits and their interrelationships, then stressed to various degrees social and occupational factors in adjustment, and then turned to intrapsychic descriptions and theories, now turns to the phenomenon that has been of concern all along — the behavior of the student — and asks directly how that behavior can be more effectively developed.

▣ PLANNING IMPROVEMENTS IN GUIDANCE SERVICES

Guidance workers are involved in many activities. These activities can be organized in daily, weekly, and annual patterns and sequences. Some of the functions served are recurrent and cyclical. These can be anticipated, ordered, and served programmatically. Other functions served are irregular, emerge spontaneously, and require activity at a high level of sensitivity and adaptability. Such activities can be preplanned only in the sense of maintaining a reserve or "stand-by" capacity. On the world scale, Dag Hammarskjold described this function as "mediating the immediate." We mourn the loss of this artist in modeling the good and reinforcing the possible and building a better world.

In most schools guidance programs have been developed to serve these two sets of functions — the regular and predictable, and the irregular and unpredictable. These are continuing and demanding responsibilities, yet they are essentially housekeeping tasks. They do not encompass a serious examination of present objectives, programs, and outcomes. They keep the present house tidy but do not plan the new one.

There are many evidences that the present house keeps the

family warm and dry but does not provide for and encourage growth. Present guidance programs tend to keep records of growth but not to encourage it. They tend to alleviate concern about problems but not to resolve them. They tend to support the acceptance of traditional goals for youth but not to discover and influence the development of new goals.

What is needed, then, is not only the continued operation of the present program but also the systematic planning of the new program. It seems to me that the central focus of a developmental guidance program for all students will be in the area of assisting individuals to accept the responsibility to make use of the right of personal decision-making. Gardner is concerned with this same point: "One of the clearest dangers in modern society is that men and women will lose the experience of participating in meaningful decisions concerning their own life and work, that they will become cogs in the machine because they *feel like* cogs in the machine."[3]

Planning for a developmental program in a realistic way will involve thinking not only of people in the field of guidance but also of people in many other disciplines. As an example of a limited approach that might yield much frustration, we could at this time deploy more of our interest to specific occupational counseling. This shift of emphasis is, in fact, taking place in many areas. Yet, unless we have a continually expanding economy that will create new jobs, vocational counseling will do little to solve the unemployment and nonemployment problem. Yet even though many of the problems are of general societal scope, there are steps that can be taken, which will improve the total guidance effort right within the schools.

Guidance Services Based on Accurate Records of Student Behaviors

A first step would involve the development of systematic plans for gathering data that would permit reasonable inferences

----

3. John Gardner, *Self Renewal: The Individual and The Innovative Society* (New York: Harper & Row, Publishers, 1964), p. 59.

to be drawn about this "wants-needs" syndrome. It is clear that the inventory of test scores as illustrated by Project Talent is a necessary but not sufficient approach. A search must be made for other meaningful data. Among areas that would appear to be fruitful are the following:

1. A systematic inventory of teacher observations of student behaviors and actions in defined learning situations is needed for both effective and ineffective behaviors. A scale needs to be developed which would utilize teacher perception beginning around the fifth grade in order to have the data available for use in the important decision-making period of the junior high school.

2. A similar instrument which gathered parent observations would include also the valuable information on parent aspiration and parent support for educational attainment.

3. Work skill competencies, as they develop in or out of school experiences, would also provide valuable data. These would include work skills developed around the house, in part-time jobs, and in other student activities of which we now have little record. Our data on students have tended to overemphasize learning in the school and to undervalue non-school learning.

4. Recent developments in the behavioral approach to modifying behavior offer interesting clues to the possibility of developing inventories of quite specific behaviors which contribute to or detract from effective learning. Exploration in this area is just getting underway and has so far tended to support the hypothesis that behavior can be modified in terms of such specific behavioral units, but we do not yet have a comprehensive pattern of behaviors whose reinforcement or extinction would enhance learning. Further exploratory work might discover behaviors which could be inventoried for a school population. With this information systematically programed, action could be undertaken.

All of this exploratory thinking on the task of planning improvements in guidance services suggests its own incompleteness. The basic form of my thinking is on the proposition that we first study the learner in his total ecology and then design our activities in accordance with our findings. It would appear that on this basis we might deploy our resources of knowledge, staff and money more effectively toward the attainment of measurable goals while protecting our clients' right and responsibility of choice in a free society.

Clear Purposes for Guidance Services

The central purpose of collecting these records of student behavior would seem to be to organize guidance needs into categories and to estimate the extent of guidance service needed for each category. Certainly, one datum long recognized as needed for planning future guidance services is information on the number of students who exhibit various kinds of behavior which impede development.

Purposes Stated as Specific Behavioral Problems Rather Than General Diagnostic Categories. Much attention in the last 20 years has been given to the subject of diagnostic categories for counseling. Pepinsky proposed eight categories as tentative groupings of the kinds of problems that counselors perceive among their clients.[4]

1. Lack of assurance.
2. Lack of information.
3. Lack of skills.
4. Dependence.
5. Cultural self-conflict.
6. Interpersonal self-conflict.
7. Intrapersonal self-conflict.
8. Choice anxiety.

It seems to me that the diagnostic category approach to improving the guidance program as a whole, and counseling in particular, is inadequate and is based upon a concept of maladjustment rather than upon concepts of adjustment and development.

----
4. H. B. Pepinsky, "The Selection and Use of Diagnostic Categories in Clinical Counseling." *Appl. Psychol. Monogr.*, 1948, No. 15, 140 pp.

Furthermore, assignment of clients to these diagnostic categories is necessarily based upon counselor judgment, clinical inference, or derivation from theory.

The approach that I am proposing starts from quite a different source. I would suggest in these inventories of student characteristics that we go back to gathering more data about the student in his total ecology, data on his own perceptions of his goals and plans for achieving these goals, data on what he does in specific situations. This is data of a more useful sort. Some approaches for inventorying student characteristics would include the following:

1. Measured aptitudes.
2. Achievement: tests and grades.
3. Teacher descriptions of student activity.
4. Parent descriptions of home activity.
5. Reports of non-school experiences.
6. Student's own statements about goals, plans, and problems.
7. Data from trained observers and camera.

We have long used such data, or at least selected elements among such data, for arranging students into groupings for teaching purposes. How can we derive, from these and other data, groupings for guidance services? As we survey our discipline at this period in history, it seems obvious that we have sufficient resources. We have personnel — numbers of trained counselors. We also have resources in knowledge, generalizations, and supporting evidence useful in developing different approaches to counseling for different kinds of student problem needs. It also seems obvious that merely increasing staff ratios, for example, increasing the number of counselors in a given school or increasing the number of dollars we are going to invest in this dimension of education, has definite limits.

Different Purposes and Services for Different Student Needs. We need to take the new attack of organizing students into groups who indicate the need for different types of guidance services and different levels of intensity of such service.

It would appear that the data concerning students in the

fifth, sixth, and seventh grades would enable us to group into one major category students who have a strong academic learning orientation. These are students who appear to have the necessary responses for school learning. They apply these learnings to the attainment of satisfactory achievement as measured by both tests and grades. Many of these students also have strong parental support for their educational attainment and strong support for their general personal development. These students may be perceived as an educationally stable group. From the counselor they will need only information on different alternatives and requirements, periodic confirmation of achievement, confirmation of plans, and reinforcement of good development.

A subcategory will consist of able students from homes where consistent parental support is *not* maintained. In these cases the students will need assistance of different kinds as they develop values, goals, and plans. In a sense what is needed here is to provide something of a parent surrogate, a reinforcing agent, for these youngsters who have low parental support.

A second major category constitutes students who do not have academic learning orientations. Here an immediate need is to identify the positive. If we had data on strengths as well as weaknesses, for example, on achievements in things other than school learning, such as work competencies achieved through non-school work experiences, certain positive evidences would emerge from student characteristics. With this kind of evidence we might break this group, and it would be a large group, into some more positively oriented categories. For example, one such subcategory would be a group that has a nonacademic learning orientation but a strong mechanical learning orientation. This is only one of many possible subgroups. With this kind of information, then, we are in a much better position to know what kinds of guidance services and what kinds of guidance information are needed as well as what kinds of student goals can be encouraged by the counselor.

I hope at this point that we are thinking of guidance as a broad array of services and of counselors as behavioral scientists. One can see the possibility of developing many different kinds of programed experiences for students. Many of these might involve a series of experiences in non-counseling activities and with people other than counselors.

■ CONCLUSION

In this paper I have attempted to highlight a problem, to be a teaser of thought, rather than to promise a solution. Certainly a solution cannot be reached by any one person. Concerted group attention by people from the guidance field and by many other people will be needed. The planning of guidance services must be based on continuing analyses of (1) the need for guidance services among the clientele to be served stated in terms of specific behavior and (2) the knowledge we have available which gives some promise of being effective in meeting student needs. Guidance purposes must be evaluatable — that is, they must indicate directly the kinds of outcomes expected so that progress toward them can be evaluated in more accurate and realistic ways.

We have talked of change, of science, physical and behavioral, and of the multitude of forces that comfort and bewilder youth.

> Restless science produces knowledge,
>   becomes an art.
> The art of the counselor touches life.
> The life of the counselor models his product.
> As he is perceived he elicits; as he perceives
>   he reinforces.
> Knowing without doing is waste.
> Doing without knowing is tyranny.
> Knowing and doing become inspiration.

CHAPTER / FIVE

Two Psychological Worlds:

AN ATTEMPTED RAPPROCHEMENT

• *C. Gilbert Wrenn,* Arizona State University

The preceding four papers have been intended to set the stage for the drama of the contest. It is clear in the political realm that if there is to be revolution there must be something to revolt against, and normally this opposition resists the invader. Unless we have a comic opera revolution there are two sides, there is a fight between them, and someone's blood is shed. The issue also is clear, someone or something must "go" in order to permit the invader's idea or person to prevail. In the intellectual world the contest is never so clearly drawn, the invader's spear is covered with a foil of qualified statements, and the well established "opposition" is inclined to say, "These are our well intentioned brothers — let us not attempt to slay, only confuse or embarass them." Often, too, the honesty of the intellectual world requires those holding the fort to admit that there is some new truth in the revolutionary position, something that will be lost if they reject it completely.

Let us see what the four papers have proposed for us. Krumboltz and Bijou are clearly the revolutionaries, the Front Bench of the Loyal Opposition, while Shoben and McDaniel represent the statesmen of the present government. The simile is sadly awry in one dimension, for neither Krumboltz on the one hand nor Shoben on the other, for example, could be thought of as members of a Conservative Party!

■ THE ATTACK

Bijou states most directly his convictions that counseling should change its course to fit the assumptions of behavioral science if it is to profit from the experimental work done this far. His four implications of behavioral science for counseling — that counseling procedures should be modified (1) to change the problem behavior directly, (2) to deal with one specific kind of behavior at a time, (3) to record problem behavior in terms of observations of frequency of occurrence, (4) to change behavior in the desired direction in small progressive steps — would indeed change the *procedures* of counseling markedly. The evidence, drawn from the work with small children with which he is so familiar, is clear and convincing. Behavior can be changed in the manner proposed. Counseling purpose as well as procedure would also be modified if his further implications are accepted: (1) that the counselor should change his emphasis in diagnosis away from commonly used tests and longitudinal data toward an understanding of present functional behavior because this will serve best and (2) that the counselor should now see himself as a behavioral engineer, one who rearranges the environment to bring about desired changes in behavior. There is little question that if the counselor desires to change specific behaviors of the kind illustrated by Bijou that he can do so — and that influencing (operating upon) the environment is an effective way of producing the change. To change his purposes takes a further step.

Krumboltz is clearly and non-dogmatically thinking directly about the counselor. In his paper he expresses the hope that behavioral science can "suggest some possible ways in which counselors and psychologists can be of greater service to their clients" (1) in conceptualizing client problems, (2) in defining client goals, (3) in selecting procedures to reach these goals and (4) in evaluating results. These are all familiar areas of concern to the counselor, couched in conventional counselor terms. When his discussion of these gets under way, however, the conventional takes on new meanings, or may be seen as openly unconventional by the practicing counselor. For counseling is to be seen in learning terms only — the counselor is "an aid in the learning process," his job is "to arrange conditions so that his client will learn more adaptive ways of coping with his difficulties." In the illustrations given a counselor would deal with a case of client shyness by using the same learning principles that would be effective in curing a slice in one's golf drive. Krumboltz would want a counselor to be warm and accepting, to believe in the client, to be concerned with client feelings. These, says Krumboltz, are necessary but not sufficient conditions; the client must still learn to resolve his difficulty, must still learn new behaviors.

Most counselors would find little disagreement with Krumboltz on client goals being seen as specific rather than global, and as unique for each client rather than general for all clients of a given class. Evidence is piling up on all sides that would question the usefulness of broad goals common to "a majority" of clients.[1] Krumboltz proposes that in (1) altering maladaptive behavior or in (2) learning the decision-making process the specific goals of the behavior to be changed are to be set by the client and agreed to by the counselor. This approaches the distinction between ends and means that Shoben alludes to and that will be developed further along in this chapter.

Under methods and procedures to meet these goals, Krumboltz proposes four approaches: (1) operant learning, (2) imitative learning or the use of behavior models, (3) cognitive learning, including the making of behavior contracts, role playing, and the timing of cues, and (4) emotional learning using classical conditioning. The case for the approaches through operant learning and cognitive learning are the most completely

---

1. See the incisive 10-year study reported by Theodore Volsky, Jr., Thomas M. Magoon, Warren T. Norman, Donald P. Hoyt, *The Outcomes of Counseling and Psychotherapy: Theory and Practice* (Minneapolis: University of Minnesota Press, 1965).

analyzed, but all four forms of learning through conditioning are said to be of value.

Only at the point of discussing evaluation does Krumboltz appear by complete denial to ignore the opposition. He rides through the open gates of the defending city on his charger, untouched by the swords of the defenders — because they are really weaponless; they *have* no swords! Current counseling procedures have no research basis, or where there is research the techniques show no measureable effect, or where there is effect it is trivial. He quotes only one research study, one in which the results are mildly negative. This ignores a fairly substantial body of research, not all of which is lacking in research finesse or negative in outcome. There can be little quarrel, on the other hand, with his contention that counseling in its totality is most difficult to measure and that one gets clearer results when the object of measurement is change in quite specific behaviors.

■ **THE DEFENSE**

McDaniel early leads a skirmish against the revolutionaries, but then he stops to parley. He is troubled because there appears to be a tendency for the behaviorists to propose that their explorations into behavior change (in animals and children, upon which there is the most research evidence, or in adolescents and adults, where there is less?) are the elements of a completed structure of action rather than hypotheses to be tested. When one considers the small number of studies on human subjects — particularly at older age levels — the hypothesis assumption appears the more reasonable of the two. McDaniel goes on to speak of the necessity of keeping to an empirical-inductive approach in which problems can be best solved if we "approach each problem in a spirit of search rather than in a spirit of communicating an answer."

McDaniel then pauses in the onward charge of his troops to agree with some of the shifts in emphasis suggested by the behaviorists (uniqueness of client problem, specificity of problem, etc.), returning to the fray only in his suggestion that the complexity of human behavior necessitates the formulation of theoretical constructs which are untested or even untestable. The inference that may be drawn from this is that the assurance of the behaviorists that their constructs are all that is needed to explain or enhance the learning process is unjustified. He then proposes a developmental program for school guidance services which focuses upon purposes stated as specific behavioral problems and upon categorization of students by type of learning need.

Shoben rolls out some big guns to the attack. They are camouflaged, to be sure, and for the first few pages they appear to search gently for the range. But the fire power becomes pinpointed about the middle of the chapter as he discusses "worth beyond utility," "education and personal worth," "private experience and personal norms," "complicity in confusing persons and things." He makes very clear that it is a mistake to assume that the power of behavioral control reveals the normative ends toward which conduct may be properly directed. The means of control does not subsume the appropriate ends to be sought. This is not a function of science, whereas the means of efficiently changing behavior toward independently conceived ends may well be a contribution of science. The proponents of any science may not assume that effective teaching or counseling is *defined* by the power to shape pupil behavior. Effective counseling may *include* this but not be defined by it. Here we might recall Krumboltz's comment that understanding is necessary but not sufficient for counseling effectiveness. In somewhat reverse order Shoben might say that skill in shaping behavior may be necessary but is not sufficient for determining counseling purpose.

It seems clear also that Shoben would propose that each man is endowed with a private self and that his sense of personal identity depends upon this. He sharply challenges the attempts of what he calls "radical empiricists and behaviorists" to shape or engineer changes in persons or societies without giving attention to the distinctive character of the person or the society. Persons possess this inner selfhood, this integrity of the unique person; things do not. To be *merely* concerned with skill in shaping is to treat a person as a thing. It is not suggested that Krumboltz or Bijou classify as Shoben's "radical behaviorists," but skill or means does seem to occupy more of their attention than purpose or ends. Krumboltz makes it clear that he would have the client determine the behavior to be changed, but this determination of ends is given scant attention in comparison to developing skill in means. Shoben would almost reverse the emphasis, saying that counselors (and educators in general) should be less concerned with the technology of fulfilling client-set goals than with critical attention to the nature of these aims, less than the *how's* than with the *what's* and the *why's*. "The engineering of behavioral means, then, while never irrelevant, seems essentially secondary to this normative function of construing ends."

Coupling scientific means with normative ends results in ambiguity — although the ever-present temptation is to seek clarity and neat structure whatever the price to be paid. The truth or falsity of normative assertions cannot be incontrovertably demonstrated because each of us extracts normative meanings from a variety of perceptions over time, meanings which may or may not be at a clear level of awareness. Ends are seldom as clear as means, nor are they arrived at by the same process. Hence the issue is joined. He who leaves ends to be assumed by the means or who gives less than primary attention to ends may be a scientist, says Shoben, but he is not one who lives up to the fundamental responsibility of educator or counselor.

■ **THE TWO WORLDS**

The differences of approach and emphasis expounded in the earlier chapters of this book are more sharply outlined when behaviorism is compared with self-psychology or phenomenology. It is common to identify these points of view with the names of Skinner and Rogers. To so restrict the comparison is unfair to many representatives of either position who are important to the development of counseling. For behaviorism, the work of Bijou and the recent work of Krumboltz would be considered as would that of Ferster, Goldiamond, Krasner, Meyerson, Bandura, Wolpe, and many others. For self theory and its application to counseling, one would look to Combs, Butler, Gendlin, Cartwright and, again, many others.[2]

It is still true, however, that the dramatic quality of the confrontation of Skinner and Rogers in their 1955 debate and upon several occasions since has focused the attention of many people upon the basic differences between the two schools of thought. In their 1962 two-day dialogue at the University of Minnesota (Duluth Branch), their several agreements and basic differences stood out clearly. Both believe in the methods of science, both depend upon research, both want to help people to change their behavior. Their procedures in the latter case differ markedly, however. Skinner would depend entirely upon sensory input to produce behavior outcomes, and Rogers would add to such input the influence of a subjective self. Skinner saw no need for such a construct, while Rogers says that he cannot explain what happens to people in therapy unless such a self is postulated. Skinner's adult (or child) is solely the product of the accidental pattern of that person's lifetime of reinforcements while Rogers assumes that a person's self also influences behavior, that each person has a *degree* of autonomy.

An analogy has occurred to me as I have read these two men and have listened to them at conferences. For Skinner (or any behaviorist, I suppose) a man operates in computer fashion in which the output of results is determined by the input of signals. Life may design the program, or parts of it may be designed by a knowing operator in the life of the man. But the computer has no autonomy — Skinner said this clearly at Duluth. Rogers (or any perceptual psychologist) would

---

2. Since writing this chapter I have "discovered" the delightful paperback entitled by T. W. Wann, *Behaviorism and Phenomenology: Contrasting Bases for Modern Psychology* (Chicago: University of Chicago Press, 1964). This symposium does not attempt an integration but provides a scholarly and lucid interchange among four psychologists, Koch, MacLeod, Skinner, and Rogers, and two philosophers, Malcolm and Scriven. The discussion comments at the conclusion of each paper are particularly entertaining and informative.

add the construct of a self which may *also* provide signals that will determine output. There is an intervening variable between receptor and effector and this has form and consistency. To Rogers this construct is essential to an understanding of at least adult behavior. To Skinner such a construct is a temporary expedient for those who find it necessary, but he finds it wholly unnecessary.

As I listened to the Duluth dialogue, a series of conversations between two men before an audience of 900 to 1,000 people, two men whose intelligence and integrity were so self-apparent, I had a feeling that "the end is not yet," that neither has more than a tentative and time-dated answer, and that each knows this. The complete assurance, sometimes bordering upon arrogance, that is occasionally displayed by the later disciples in each school of thought was almost entirely lacking in this dialogue. Each was still searching, each still humble with an acute awareness of his small stock of even relatively final answers. I also ruminated that Rogers might have been more like Skinner had he worked with animals as much as had Skinner, and that the subjective self might be more reasonable to Skinner had he engaged in therapy with people as long as had Rogers. In fact each might be said to be the product of the reinforcements made possible by the particular subjects with which he had worked! Skinner with a lifetime of adult therapy might not be the same Skinner, nor Rogers with animals so sure of the subjective self.

Another encounter of considerable interest to an audience at the 1965 American Personnel and Guidance Association Annual Convention was the presentation on the implications for counseling of perceptual psychology by Arthur Combs and a similar argument for behaviorism by John Krumboltz. Combs made clear that perceptual psychology was almost "synonomous with a psychology of meanings," and that all behavior is a function of the meanings of the situation to the individual at the instant of behavior. This is the perceptual field of the person at that time. The emphasis is on the present. The past is important only as it influences the person's present perceptions. People can be helped without either counselor or client understanding how perceptions are arrived at. The only reality is the present perceptions. Charles Combs, brother of Arthur, recently put it this way: "Human behavior, then, is a function not of 'fact' as a determiner but *of our ideas* about ourselves and about the world in which we exist at any instant. . . . The past exists only in its representations in the present phenomenal field. . . . To the phenomenologist, fact is dynamic, temporal and most of all, illusory. While it has the quality of reality in the eye of the beholder, its reality is *only* that of the beholder, or partially that of those who share his field."[3] Arthur Combs sees the basic motivation as being the individual's need for self-organization. Everyone is *always* motivated in terms of what he sees as enhancing his own self.

Krumboltz would apparently see little of this as essential for changing behavior. What is essential is to discover and apply some basic principles of learning since most of the important human behaviors (including the development of behavior theories!) are learned. As an illustration he provided a classically simple statement of one basic principle of operant learning: "A person can learn a new behavior pattern if successive approximations (or movements) toward it are reinforced." There is no need for recourse to a rather shadowy phenomenal field or a construct of self-awareness. Yet the desire to help, to free the individual, may be as great as in perceptual therapy. "Reinforcement can help people to develop behaviors they want to develop and thus increase their freedom by increasing their repertoire of behaviors."

■ INTEGRATION FOR THE PRACTICING COUNSELOR

There is little to be gained by attempting to force agreement when none is suggested or even wanted by either side. And currently few in either school of thought are worrying about the other. What distresses me is that some are entirely

----
3. This is quoted from a letter written in response to an appeal from the writer to "help me explain perceptual psychology simply to English audiences!"

willing to assume the other side is all wrong, and will come to its senses sooner or later. If not, then, each would say that we have our work to do, let's be about it and not worry about the opposition. This may be satisfactory for the theoretician or even for research workers who are not aware of the blinders they are wearing, or who find that wearing them is not uncomfortable — it may even be fashionable! The rub comes for the practicing counselor. Must he accept one approach and reject the other? Most college professors will encourage him to do so — it makes lectures easier to organize and research projects easier to design. But is he losing something by being thus "consistent," is he throwing out the baby with the dirty bath water?

The distinction between means and ends has been hinted at several times in earlier chapters and recapitulated in this chapter. It is a significant difference and one that I think practicing counselors can utilize. The "therapeutic contract" has also been mentioned. It would seem to me that perceptual or integrative or self-psychology can contribute to the examination and determination of meaningful ends or purposes of a given counseling relationship, and that scientific behaviorism (most importantly, perhaps, operant conditioning) can contribute a significant method for producing desired change in behavior or attitude. If it is clear that the *client* is to select his own ends, that it is his life, not the counselor's, then the client is safe in agreeing that the counselor is to use his professional judgment and skill in selecting and using the means that will help him, the client, reach those ends. He does not need to know what is happening to make the relationship productive if he trusts the judgment and integrity of the counselor. (Nor, incidentally, does this seem too necessary in straight perceptual psychotherapy.) There is nothing ethically awry about counselor choice and operation of means if there is equal adherence to the inherent right of the client to decide *what* he wants to change — or to be. I am a little weary of having my friends in one camp look askance at me because I insist that there is virtue *also* in the "opposite" position — that our profession is not composed of Good Guys and Bad Guys. Pure White and pure Black are rather hard to find. I must trust the other person's good will as much as I trust my own — sometimes more because I know "me" so much better than "him"!

There is also much to be gained from the behaviorist's insistence that *if counseling outcomes are to be measured* we must work with specific behaviors. We have too long deluded ourselves that global outcomes must be assumed for the counseling relationship since the counselor is dealing with a global or integrated organism. This conclusion does not follow from the earlier presumption. We *have* specific behaviors and changing them may be a specific operation, and *what is to be changed* at a given time is unique to the person. In this connection, however, it is not necessary to conclude that *all* counseling outcomes are to be measured. Sometimes the outcome is an important but unplanned-for by-product. Sometimes there must be resolution of a disorganized total pattern of living into something *recognizable by the client* before specific outcomes can be conceptualized and sought by him.

The other side of the coin is implied in the comment just preceding on nonanalyzable but significant outcomes. The human being is more than a reacting organism, he is an integrating organism, and until more evidence is accumulated, we must assume that this integration has a consistency which is meaningful to that individual. How he perceives himself and others is a significant factor in how he responds to stimuli and situations. The counselor would do well to follow this lead in helping the client to evaluate the reality-orientation of the goals he may set for himself, even of the behavior he wishes changed. The end may well demand more attention than the means, as Shoben insists. And here I think that the integrative, perceptual, dynamically oriented approach can help the counselor more than can the behavioral scientist approach. Counseling involves, or perhaps is, a learning process, but the content material of the learning is the learner, not something exterior to him. And this adds to the learning process an element of individualized meanings of self and world.

A closing comment, but by no means a conclusion, is more than half seriously suggested by a recent experience of mine in coding responses to two protocols for use in teaching. I used the letter "R" to indicate a "reflection" response and then used the same letter in another approach to a core analysis to indicate a "reinforcement" response. It was confusing to the students! Further attention to the code letter, however, suggested that perhaps reflection *is* a reinforcement.[4] When a counselor reflects feeling, he is encouraging the client to move further in the same direction *if* his needs demand this. The counselor is reinforcing what he considers psychological movement that is meaningful to the client. If one perceives that the slogan of one school of thought and action in counseling is not the complete antithesis of the slogan of the other school, then integration seems a little more possible.

Perhaps it is not integration that is to be sought at all but *selective use* of elements, whatever the source. The counselor deals with a *person* who wants *changes,* and the counselor's responsibility goes beyond the intellectual stages of dealing with ideas and with disembodied facts. May I quote again from Charles Combs' recent letter to me. "It seems to me," he writes, "that all psychologies from totemism and animism to behaviorism, psychoanalysis, and phenomenonological existentialism, or those that are soon to come, seek to explain and predict the human phenomenon. The differences lie in how much of and the nature of the phenomenon that we choose to countenance as worthy of consideration." To him, of course, phenomenonological existentialism is "the present-most-inclusive frame of reference." Others whom I respect would make a different selection. But most of all note Combs' reference to "those that are soon to come" and the *"present* most inclusive."[5] There will be a next step and a next. Truth is forever emerging, never completely found. Will the next step include both of the "R's"? I think so.

----

4. This is clearly suggested in the study reported by Charles B. Truax, "Reinforcement and Nonreinforcement in Rogerian Psychotherapy." *J. abnorm. Psychol.,* 1966, 71, 1-9.

5. Fred S. Keller, in commenting as a behaviorist upon an early version of this manuscript, observed that the treatment was "sympathetic and generous with respect to both viewpoints" and that this was a real service "especially for the audience in question and *at this stage of our development."*

APPENDIX

Demonstrations and Discussions
at the 1965 Cubberley Conference

■ DEMONSTRATIONS

1. *Encouraging College Accomplishment among Disadvantaged Youth* (Leader: Carl E. Thoresen, Assistant Professor, College of Education, Michigan State University, East Lansing, Michigan).

Description: Sample of interviews between a counselor and a Negro student illustrating how immediate rewards were "paid" for successful college work. Reactions of counselor, teachers, tutors, and the student himself.

2. *Minimizing Classroom Learning and Discipline Problems* (Leaders: Dwight L. Goodwin, School Psychologist, San Carlos Elementary School District, San Carlos, California; Jean Yoder, Elementary Teacher, Palo Alto, California).

Description: Sample interview showing how a psychologist can assist a teacher in managing selected discipline and learning problems by focusing attention on conditions which typically precede and follow incidents of the problem behavior.

3. *Developing Decision-Making Ability* (Leader: William W. Yabroff, Research Consultant, Palo Alto Unified School District, Palo Alto, California).

Description: Example of a presentation using instructional materials to help each student learn the process of making decisions and estimating his own chances of success in high school and in different colleges.

4. *Behavior Therapy with an Autistic Child* (Leader: Gerald C. Davison, Assistant Professor, Department of Psychology, State University of New York at Stony Brook, Long Island).

Description: Filmed example of how a severely disturbed child learns to follow instructions during a short period of reinforcement. Discussion of rationale for changes in behavior.

5. *Reducing Test Anxiety* (Leader: John Emery, Counseling Psychologist, Student Counseling Service, University of California at Davis).

Description: Example of systematic desensitization to reduce fear of taking examinations.

6. *Promoting an Environment Conducive to Elementary School Achievement* (Leaders: Laurence Horowitz, Psychologist; Marge Bonetti, Elementary Teacher, Mt. Diablo Unified School District, Concord, California).

Description: Demonstration of psychologist-teacher interviews to develop a reinforcement schedule to help a hyperactive, underachieving third-grade boy.

7. *Increasing Attentive Behavior* (Leader: Stewart Nixon, Stanford University).

Description: Demonstration of remote-controlled experimental equipment and techniques used to increase the attentive task-oriented behavior of hyperactive children.

8. *Promoting an Environment Conducive to Secondary School Achievement* (Leaders: Laurence Horowitz, Psychologist; Ray Enjaian, Counselor; Ken Davis and William Rothlisberger, Intermediate Teachers, Mt. Diablo Unified School District, Concord, California).

Description: Demonstration of psychologist-teacher interviews to develop a reinforcement schedule to help an under-achieving 14-year-old boy overcome his failure orientation.

9. *Encouraging Career Exploration through Programed Learning Materials* (Leader: Fern Bruner, Counseling Psychologist, Palo Alto Unified School District, Palo Alto, California).

Description: Presentation of programed booklets designed to stimulate deliberation about career plans by high school students.

10. *Treating Autistic Children* (Leader: Ivar Lovaas, Assistant Professor of Psychology, University of California at Los Angeles).

Description: Filmed and tape-recorded examples of procedures used to establish social and intellectual behaviors in autistic children.

11. *Improving Test-Wiseness* (Leader: B. Gordon Gibb, Associate Professor of Psychology, Chico State College, Chico, California).

Description: Presentation of materials which have helped college students develop the test-taking skills which enable them to compete on a more equal basis with test-wise students.

12. *Helping Underachievers by the Use of Social Models* (Leader: Alice Beach, Psychologist, Jefferson Unified School District, Santa Clara, California).

Description: Excerpts from seven model interviews, each designed to develop one type of useful achievement-oriented behavior (e.g., how to ask the teacher a sensible and precise question). Reactions of counselors who have used the model tapes.

13. *Stimulating Interest in Career Exploration* (Leader: Lawrence E. Sheppard, Director of Research and Guidance, Jefferson Elementary School District, Daly City, California).

Description: Example of materials which stimulate interest by allowing students to solve problems like those solved by members of various occupations.

14. *Behavioral Techniques in Child-Rearing* (Leader: Marcia McBeath, Stanford University).

Description: Examples of methods for increasing the amount of practice on a musical instrument, improving poor eating habits, establishing persistence, and allaying a fear of animals.

15. *Family Group Consultation* (Leaders: Daniel W. Fullmer, Director of Development and Evaluation and Professor of Psychology; Earl T. Zwetschke, Associate Professor of Psychology, Oregon State System of Higher Education, Portland, Oregon).

Description: Demonstration in which one or more families interact with the counselor and each other to help resolve intra-family concerns.

16. *Counseling by Computer* (Leaders: John W. Loughary, Associate Research Professor, Teaching Research Division, Oregon State System of Higher Education, Eugene, Oregon; John Cogswell and Donald Estaven, Human Factors Scientists, Systems Development Corporation, Santa Monica, California).

Description: Filmed description of AUTOCOUN: an experimentally operational, computer-based counseling simulation system. Sample "interviews" between pupils and computer.

17. *Behavioral Counseling with Shy Children* (Leader: Clarence J. Johnson, Director, Special Services, Rio Linda School District, Rio Linda, California).

Description: Sample interviews in which the counselor reinforces the verbal responses of shy children. Reactions of children and counselor.

18. *Improving Study Habits by Reinforcement Counseling* (Leader: T. Antoinette Ryan, Associate Professor, College of Education, Oregon State University, Corvallis, Oregon).

Description: Example of counselor's use of reinforcement to develop more efficient study behavior.

19. *Stimulating Career Exploration and Class Participation* (Leader: Carl E. Thoresen, Assistant Professor, College of Education, Michigan State University, East Lansing, Michigan).

Description: Samples of tape-recorded model interviews (representing various levels of athletic and academic success) to be used with students of different success levels.

■ INFORMAL SEMINARS

1. *Interests and Values: Are They Changeable?* (Leader: Frank M. Fletcher, President, Division of Counseling Psychology, American Psychological Association; and Professor of Psychology, The Ohio State University, Columbus, Ohio).

2. *Technological Change: Its Significance for Counseling* (Leader: Henry Borow, Professor of Psychological Studies, University of Minnesota, Minneapolis, Minnesota).

3. *Implications of the Behavioral Sciences for the Role and Preparation of the Elementary Counselor* (Leader: Marjorie Mottishaw Anderson, Chairman, Western Association of Counselor Educators and Supervisors, and State Supervisor of Guidance and Counseling, Olympia, Washington).

4. *Techniques for the In-Service Training of Counselors* (Leader: Dale C. Burklund, President, California Counseling and Guidance Association, and Director, Guidance and Curriculum, Santa Clara County Office of Education, San Jose, California).

5. *Guidance Services: Passive Referrals or Active Intervention* (Leader: Walter Lauterbach, President, California Association of School Psychologists and Psychometrists).

INDEX